RESEARCH METHODOLOGY

RESEARCH METHODOLOGY

P. Sam Daniel

and

Aroma G Sam

Research Methodology

P. Sam Daniel, Aroma G Sam

ISBN: 978-81-7835-900-7

Kalpaz Publications

C-30, Satyawati Nagar

Delhi-110052

E-mail : Kalpaz@hotmail.com

Leser Type setting : Lucky Graphic, Delhi

Printed at : Chowla Offset Press, Delhi

Dedicated to Our Parents

Mrs. Devanesam Ponniah & Mr. Daniel Ponniah

and

Mrs. Annammal Chelliah & Mr. John Chelliah

Who Dedicated

Their Service for the Cause of Education

CONTENTS

FOREWORD

Dr Pon Kothandaraman-Portko

Former Vice-Chencellor of the University of Madras

Saalbu Maaligai

Plot No. 41, Sankarapuram First Street, Sithalapakkam

Chennai 600073, Tamilnadu, India

It was a pleasure for me to go through the volume entitled Research Methodology authored by Dr. P Sam Daniel and Dr Aroma G Sam. All though the major area of Research Methodolgy is common for all disciplines, there are minor variations in the methodology from one discipline to another. The auothrs of this volume have gained a rich experience in research such and teaching. The present volume elabortory deals with many impor-tant areas of research such as research kinds, research processes, research design, data collection, analysis, interpretation and thesis writing.

Any researcher who carefully goes through this volume will find it immensely useful for his research. We need a number of advisory volumes of this kind for our young researchers so as to cater to their needs in different areas of research. The supervisors and profes-sional researchers also will get benefited by this rich volume. By producing this volume the authors have done a good servie to the world of research. I wish the authors a good success in all similar ventures in future.

Chennai 126 Pon Kothadaraman

29th December, 2010

PREFACE

The importance of research has gained momentum in the present century. The range of possibilities and changes in methodologies often confuse, rather than clarify, the researcher. Most of the books on Research Methodology are detailed and technical, making their occasional use impractical. Research Methodology should be a helpful aid summarizing basic information drawn from several key sources.

It should be coulmination of useful methods and techniques as a pool of guidelines, selected from various references on research design, methods, strategies, statistical techniques and analysis of data, guideline for research proposal, report, thesis or article. It should be a refresher to the individual who is not familiar with current trends on methods and techniques in this area. It should function as a checking and comparing aid for the researcher to ensure that he has taken into account the important considerations, correctly weighed the advantages and limitations among alternatives and has placed himself in the strongest position to reach useful and defensive conclusions.

Both the authors have rich experience in various universities both in India and abroad, teaching Research Methodology and guiding M.Phil., M.Th., Ph.D, and other doctoral scholars for more than forty years and produced many Ph.D. Scholars. The experience they gained through their teaching and research has culminated into the writing of the book "Research Methodology".

During the preparation of this book, to bring together concerns, ideas and concepts from different sources over an extended period of times, the final responsibility of the work and its judgment about the contents and any errors rest with the authors. Our gratitude to Mr. John D Kesari for his valuable comments while going through the draft of the book.

We would like to express our indebtedness to Dr. Ken Gnanakan,

President, ACTS Group of Institutions, Bangalore and Dr. Richard Gnanakan, Principal, ACTS Academy of Higher Education, Bangalore for their encouragement. We thank Rev. G. James, ACTS Academy of Higher Education, and Mrs.Vimala Rajagopal, for carrying out the editorial work.

Dr. Aroma G Sam **Dr. P Sam Daniel**

1

RESEARCH METHODOLOGY: AN INTRODUCTION

Meaning of Research

Research refers to a search for knowledge. One can define research as a scientific and systematic search for pertinent information on a specific topic. In fact, research is an art of scientific investigation. Research is an academic activity and as such, the term should be used in a technical sense. Research comprises of defining and redefining problems, formulating a hypothesis or suggested solutions; collecting, organizing and evaluating data, making deductions and reaching conclusions; and finally carefully testing the conclusions to determine whether they fit the formulating hypothesis.

Research is, thus, an original contribution to the existing stock of knowledge for further enrichment. It is the pursuit of truth with the help of study, observation, comparison and experiment. In short, the search for knowledge through objective and systematic method of finding solutions to a problem is Research. The systematic approach concerning generalization and formulation of a theory is also termed as Research.

Objectives of Research

The purpose of research is to discover answers to questions through the application of scientific procedures. The main aim of research is to find out the truth which is hidden and which has not been discovered as yet. Though, each research study has its own specific purpose, we may think of research objectives as falling into a number of broad groups namely:

1. To gain familiarity with a phenomenon or to achieve new insights into it (studies with this object in view are termed as

exploratory or formulative research studies); e.g., Influence of Globalization.

2. To portray accurately, the characteristics of a particular individual, situation or a group (studies with this object in view are known as descriptive research studies): e.g., Writing a Descriptive Grammar.
3. To determine the frequency with which something occurs or with which it is associated (studies with this object in view are known as diagnostic research studies), e.g., Population Studies.
4. To test a hypothesis of a causal relationship between variables (such studies are known as hypothesis – testing research studies), e.g., Literacy and related Empowerments.

Motivation in Research

What makes people to undertake research? This is a question of fundamental importance.

The possible motives for doing research may be either one or more of the following:

1. Desire to get a research degree along with its consequential benefits: e.g., M.Phil., M.Th., Ph.D.
2. Desire to face the challenge in solving an unsolved problem, i.e. concern over practical problems initiates research, e.g., Finding remedies for AIDS.
3. Desire to get intellectual joy of doing some creative work, e.g., Creative writing, life long learning.
4. Desire to be of service to society, e.g., Dealing with socio-economic problems.
5. Desire to get respectability, e.g., To adore with titles, Doctor or Master.

These are some of the list of factors motivating people to undertake research studies. Many more factors such as directives of government, employment conditions, curiosity about new things, desire to understand casual relationships, social thinking and awakening, and the like may as well motivate (or at times compel) people to perform research operations.

Importance of Knowing How Research is Done

The study of research methodology gives the scholar the necessary training in gathering materials and arranging or card–indexing them, participation in the field work when required, and also training in techniques for the collection of data appropriate to particular problems, in the use of statistics, questionnaire and controlled experimentation and in recording evidence, sorting it out and interpreting it. In fact, importance of knowing the methodology of research or how research is done stems from the following considerations:

1. For one who is preparing himself for a career of carrying out research, the importance of knowing research methodology and research techniques are obvious since the same constitute the tools of his trade. The knowledge of methodology provides good training especially to the new research worker and enables him to do better research. It helps him to develop disciplined thinking or a bent of mind to observe the field objectively. Hence, those aspiring for careerism in research must develop the skill of using research techniques and must thoroughly understand the logic behind them.

2. Knowledge of how to do research will inculcate the ability to evaluate and use research results with reasonable confidence. In other words, one can take the knowledge of research methodology as helpful in various fields such as government or business administration, community development and social work, where persons are increasingly called upon to evaluate and use research results for action.

3. When one knows how research is done, then one may have the satisfaction of acquiring a new intellectual tool which can become a way of looking at the world and of judging every day experience. Accordingly, it enables them to make intelligent decisions concerning problems facing them in practical life at different points of time. Thus, the knowledge of research methodology provides tools to look at things in life objectively.

4. In this scientific age, all researchers are in many ways

consumers of research results and they can use them intelligently provided we are able to judge the adequacy of the methods by which they have been obtained. The knowledge of methodology helps the consumer of research results to evaluate them and enables to take rational decisions.

Research Approaches/Methods

The different types of research brings to light the fact that there are two basic approaches to research, viz., quantitative approach and the qualitative approach. The former involves the generation of data in quantitative form, which can be subjected to rigorous quantitative analysis in a formal and rigid fashion. This approach can be further sub – classified into inferential, experimental and simulation approaches to research. The purpose of inferential approach to research is to form a data base from which to infer characteristics or relationships of population. This usually means survey research where a sample of population is studied (questioned or observed) to determine its characteristics, and it is then inferred that the population has the same characteristics. Example; Total populations being 5 lakhs (universe), a sample of 500 persons are selected by using random sampling method for the study.

Experimental approach is characterized by much greater control over the research environment and in this case some variables are manipulated to observe their effect on other variables. Example; For a particular group of people, age is kept as an independent variable; weight, height, education, intelligence, employment are kept as dependent variables. Simulation approach involves the construction of an artificial environment within which relevant information and data can be generated. This permits an observation of the dynamic behavior of a system (or its sub - system) under controlled conditions. The term 'simulation' in the context of business and social sciences applications refers to "the operation of a numerical model that represents the structure of a dynamic process. Given the values of initial conditions, parameters and exogenous variables, a simulation is run to represent the structure of a dynamic process. Given the values of initial conditions, parameters and exogenous variable, a simulation is run to represent the behavior of the process over time. Simulation approach can also be useful in building models for understanding future conditions. Example: Political parties giving incentives to attract the voters, rewards given to best students.

Qualitative approach to research is concerned with subjective assessment of attitudes, opinions and behaviour. Research in such a situation is a function of researcher's insights and impressions. Such an approach to research generates results either in non – quantitative form or in the form which is not subjected to rigorous quantitative analysis.

Table 1.1

Nine Basic Methods of Research

Method	*Purpose*
Historical	To reconstruct the past objectively and accurately, often in relation to the tenability of an hypothesis.
Descriptive	To describe systematically a situation or area of interest factually and accurately.
Development	To investigate patterns and sequences of growth and / or change as a function of time.
Case and Field	To study intensively the background, current status, and environmental interactions of a given social unit; an individual, group, institution, or community.
Correlational	To investigate the extent to which variations in one factor correspond with variations in one or more other factors based on correlation coefficients.
Casual-Comparative or "Ex Post Facto"	To investigate possible cause – and – effect relationships by observing some existing consequence and searching back through the data for plausible casual factors.
True Experimental	To investigate possible cause-and-effect relationships by exposing one or more

	experimental groups to one or more treatment conditions and comparing the results to one or more control groups not receiving the treatment (random assignment being essential).
Quasi-Experimental	To approximate the conditions of the true experiment in a setting which does not allow the control and / or manipulation of all relevant variables. The researcher must clearly understand what compromises exist in the internal and external validity of his design and proceed within these limitations.
Action	To develop new skills or new approaches and to solve problems with direct application to the class room or other applied setting.

Source: Issac & Michael, 1982.

Examples

Population census studies, public opinion surveys, fact-finding surveys, status studies, task analysis studies, questionnaire and interview studies, observation studies, job descriptions, surveys of literature, documentary analyses, anecdotal records, critical incident reports, test score analyses, and normative data. A longitudinal growth study following an initial sample of 200 children from six months of age to adulthood; a cross-sectional growth study investigating changing patterns of intelligence by sampling groups of children at ten different age levels; a trend study projecting the future growth and educational needs of a community from past trends and recent building estimates.

The case history of a child with an above average IQ but with severe learning disabilities; an intensive study of a group of teenage youngsters on probation for drug abuse; an intensive study of a typical suburban community in terms of its socio-economic characteristics.

To investigate relationships between reading achievement scores and one or more other variables of interest; a factor-analytic study of several intelligence tests; a study to predict success in college based on inter correlation patterns between college grades and selected high school variables.

To identify factors related to the "drop-out" problem in a particular high school using data from records over the period of ten years; to investigate similarities and differences between such groups as smokers and nonsmokers, readers and nonreaders, or delinquents and nondelinquents, using data on file.

To investigate the effectiveness of three methods, i.e., listening, reading and writing, to first grade children using random assignments of children and teachers to groups and methods; to investigate the effects of a specific tranquilizing drug on the learning behavior of boys identified as "hyperactive" using random assignment to groups receiving three different levels of the drug and two control groups with and without.

Most so-called field experiments, operational research and even the more sophisticated forms of action research which attempt to get at causal factors in real life settings where only partial control is possible; e.g., an investigation of the effectiveness of any method or treatment condition where random assignment of subjects to methods or conditions is not possible.

An in-service training program to help teachers develop new skills in facilitating class discussions; to experiment with new approaches to teaching reading to bilingual children; to develop more effective counseling techniques for underachievers.

Basic Steps in the Planning and Conduct of Research

1. Identify the problem area.
2. Survey the literature relating to it.
3. Define the actual problem for investigation in clear, specific terms.
4. Formulate testable hypotheses and define the basic concepts and variables.
5. State the underlying assumptions which govern the interpretation of results.
6. Construct the research design to maximize internal and external validity.

(a) Selection of subjects.

(b) Control and / or manipulation of relevant variables.

(c) Establishment of criteria to evaluate outcomes.

(d) Instrumentation – Selection or development of the criterion measures.

7. Specify the data collection procedures.
8. Select the data analysis methodology.
9. Execute the research plan.
10. Evaluate the results and draw conclusions.

Historical Research

Example

To study the dynasty of the famous Chola Kingdom in Tamilnadu would include its administration in the past and its relevance to the present and to test the hypothesis that "Adult franchise in the form of using palm leaf is a heritage legacy of democracy in Tamil Nadu".

Characteristics

1. Historical research depends upon data observed by others rather than by the investigator. Good data result from painstaking detective work which analyzes the authenticity, accuracy and significance of source material.
2. Contrary to popular notions, historical research must be rigorous, systematic, and exhaustive; much "research" claiming to be historical is an undisciplined collection of inappropriate, unreliable, or biased information.
3. Historical research depends upon two kinds of data: Primary sources where the author was a direct observer of the recorded event, and secondary sources where the author is reporting the observation of others and is or more times removed from the original event. Of the two, primary sources carry the authority of firsthand evidence and have priority in data collection.
4. Two basic forms of criticism weigh the value of the data:

external criticism which asks, "Is the document or relic authentic?" and internal criticism which asks, "If authentic, are the data accurate and relevant?" Internal criticism must examine the motives, biases, and limitations of the author which might cause him to exaggerate, restrict, or overlook information. This critical evaluation of the data is what makes true historical research so rigorous-in many ways, more demanding than experimental methods.

5. While historical research is similar to the "reviews of the literature" which precede other forms of research, the historical approach is more exhaustive, seeking out information from a larger array of sources. It also tracks down information that is much older than required by most reviews and hunts for unpublished material not cited in the standard references.

Steps

1. Define the problem. The researcher should ask these questions: Is the historical approach best suited for this problem? Are pertinent data available? Will the findings be educationally significant?
2. State the research objectives and, if possible, the hypothesis that will give direction and focus to the research.
3. Collect the data, keeping in mind the distinction between primary and secondary sources. An important skill in historical research ie note-taking small file cards (3x5, 4x6), each containing one item of information and coded by topic which are easy to rearrange and convenient to file.
4. Evaluate the data, applying both internal and external criticism.
5. Report the findings, including a statement of the problem, a review of source material, a statement of underlying assumptions, basic hypothesis, and methods used to test the hypotheses, the findings obtained, the interpretations and conclusions reached, and a bibliography.

Descriptive Research

The purpose of descriptive research is to describe systematically the facts and characteristics of a given population or area of interest, factually and accurately.

Examples

1. A public opinion survey to assess the pre-election status of voter attitudes in a state election.
2. A community survey to establish the needs for a vocational education program.
3. A study and definition of all personnel position in an education center.
4. A report of test score results in a school district.

Characteristics

1. Descriptive research is used in the literal sense of describing situations or events. It is the accumulation of a data base that is solely descriptive it does not necessarily seek or explain relationships, test hypotheses, make predictions, or get at meanings and implications, although research aimed at these more powerful purposes may incorporate descriptive methods. Research authorities, however, are not in agreement on what constitutes "descriptive research" and often broaden the term to include all forms of research except historical and experimental. In this broader context, the term survey studies is often used to cover the examples listed above.
2. Purpose of Survey Studies
   (a) To collect detailed factual information that describes existing phenomena.
   (b) To identify problems or justify current conditions and practices.
   (c) To make comparisons and evaluations.
   (d) To determine what others are doing with similar problems or situations and benefit from their experience in making future plans and decisions.

Steps

1. Define the objectives in clear, specific terms. What facts and characteristics are to be uncovered?

2. Design the approach. How will the data be collected? How will the subjects be selected to ensure they represent the population to be described? What instruments or observation techniques are available or what will he needed to be developed? Will the data collection methods need to be field-tested and will data gatherers need to be trained?
3. Collect the data.
4. Report the results, (Van Daren, 1979).

Developmental Research

The purpose of development research is to investigate patterns and sequences of growth and / or change as a function of time.

Examples

1. Longitudinal growth studies directly measuring the nature and rate of changes in a sample of the same children at different stages of development.
2. Cross-sectional growth studies indirectly measuring the nature and rate of these same changes by drawing samples of different children from representative age levels.
3. Trend studies designed to establish patterns of change in the past in order to predict future patterns or conditions.

Characteristics

1. Developmental research focuses on the study of variables and their development over a period of months or years. It asks, "What are the patterns of growth, their rates, their directions, their sequences and the interrelated factors affecting these characteristics?"
2. The sampling problem in the longitudinal method is complicated by the limited number of subjects it can follow over the years; any selective factor affecting attrition biases the longitudinal study. If the threat of attrition is avoided by sampling from a stable population, this introduces unknown biases associated with such populations. Further more, once underway, the longitudinal method does not lend itself to

improvements in techniques without losing the continuity of the procedure. Finally, this method requires the continuity of staff and financial support over an extended period of time and typically is confined to university or foundation centers that can maintain such an effort.

3. Cross-sectional studies usually include more subjects, but describe fewer growth factors than longitudinal studies. While the latter is the only direct method of studying human development, the cross-sectional approach is less expensive and faster since the actual passage of time is eliminated by sampling different subjects across age ranges. Sampling in the cross-sectional method is complicated because the same children are not involved at each age level and may not be comparable. To generalize intrinsic developmental patterns from these sequential samples of children runs the risk of confusing differences due to development with other differences between the groups that are artifacts of the sampling process.
4. Trend studies are vulnerable to unpredictable factors that modify or invalidate trends based on the past. In general, long-range prediction is an educated guess while short-range prediction is more reliable and valid.

Steps

1. Define the problem or state the objectives.
2. Review the literature to establish a baseline of existing information and to compare research methodologies including available instruments and data collection techniques.
3. Design the approach.
4. Collect the data.
5. Evaluate the data and report the results.

Case and Field Study Research

The purpose of case and field study research is to study intensively the background, current status and environmental inter-actions of a given social unit: an individual, group, institution or community.

Examples

1. Piaget's studies of cognitive growth in children.
2. An in-depth study of a pupil with a learning disability by a school psychologist or a student on probation by a social worker.
3. An intensive study of the "inner city" culture and living conditions in a large metropolitan environment.
4. An anthropologist's exhaustive field study of cultural life on a remote Indian reservation in the Andaman & Nichobar Islands, Union Territories of Government of India.

Characteristics

1. Case studies are in-depth investigations of a given social unit resulting in a complete, well-organized picture of that unit. Depending upon the purpose, the scope of the study may encompass an entire life cycle or only a selected segment; it may concentrate upon specific factors or take in the totality of elements and events.
2. Compared to a survey study which tends to examine a small number of variables across a large sample of units, the case study tends to examine a small number of units across a large number of variables and conditions.

Strengths

1. Case studies are particularly useful as background information for planning major investigations in the social sciences. Because they are intensive, they bring to light the important variables, processes and interactions that deserve more extensive attention. They pioneer new ground and often are the source of fruitful hypotheses for further study.
2. Case study data provide useful anecdotes or examples to illustrate more generalized statistical findings.

Weakness

1. Because of their narrow focus on a few units, case studies are limited in their representativeness. They do not allow valid

generalization to the population from which their units came until the appropriate follow-up research is accomplished, focusing on specific hypothesis and using proper sampling methods.

2. Case studies are particularly vulnerable to subjective biases. The case itself may be selected because of its dramatic, rather than typical, attributes; or because it neatly fits the researchers preconceptions. To the extent selective judgments rule certain data in or out, or assign a high or low value to their significance, or place them in one context rather than another, subjective interpretation is influencing the outcome.

Steps

1. State the objectives. What is the unit of study and what characteristics, relationships and processes will direct the investigation?
2. Design the approach. How will the units be selected? What sources of data are available? What data collection methods will be used?
3. Collect the data.
4. Organize the information to form a coherent, well-integrated reconstruction of the unit of study.
5. Report the results and discuss their significance.

Correlational Research

The Purpose of correlational research is to investigate the extent to which variations in one factor correspond with variations in one or more other factors based on correlation coefficients.

Examples

1. A study investigating the relationship between grade point average as the criterion variable and a number of other variables of interest.
2. A factor-analytic study of several personality tests.
3. A study to predict success in graduate school based on intercorrelation patterns for undergraduate variables.

Characteristics

1. Appropriate where variables are very complex and / or do not lend themselves to the experimental method and controlled manipulation.
2. Permits the measurement of several variables and their interrelationships simultaneously and in a realistic setting.
3. Gets at the degrees of relationship rather than the all or nothing question posed by experimental design: "Is an effect present or absent?"
4. Among its limitations are the following:
   (a) It only identifies what goes with what – it does not necessarily identify cause and effect relationships.
   (b) It is less rigorous than the experimental approach because it exercises less control over the independent variables.
   (c) It is prone to identify spurious relational patterns or elements which have little or no reliability or validity.
   (d) The relational patterns are often arbitrary and ambiguous.
   (e) It encourages a "shot-gun" approach to research, indiscriminately throwing in data from miscellaneous sources and defying any meaningful or useful interpretation.

Steps

1. Define the problem.
2. Review the literature.
3. Design the approach.
4. Collect the data.
5. Analyze and interpret the results.

Casual – Comparative Research

The purpose of casual comparative research is to investigate possible cause and effect relationships by observing some existing consequence and searching back through the data for plausible casual factors. This is in contrast to the experimental method which collects its data under controlled conditions in the present.

Examples

1. To identify factors characterizing persons having either high or low accident rates, using data in insurance company records.
2. To determine the attributes of effective teachers as defined, for example, by their performance, evaluations and other data in the personal files. Teacher's records over the past ten years are then examined, comparing these data to the amount of orientation / refresher courses attendance or to each of several other factors.
3. To look for patterns of behaviour and achievement associated with age difference at the time of school entrance, using descriptive data on behaviour and achievement test scores in the cumulative pupil records of children currently in S.S.L.C.

Casual comparative research "ex post facto" in nature, which means the data are collected after all the events of interest have occurred. The investigator then takes one or more effects (dependent variables) and examines the data by going back through time, seeking out causes, relationships and their meanings.

Strengths

1. The casual comparative method is appropriate in many circumstances where the more powerful experimental method is not possible.
   (a) When it is not always possible to select, control and manipulate the factors necessary to study cause and effect relations directly.
   (b) When the control of all variations except a single independent variable may be highly unrealistic and artificial, preventing the normal interaction with other influential variables.
   (c) When laboratory controls for many research purposes would be impractical, costly or ethically questionable.

Note: The experimental method involves both an experimental and a control group. Some treatment, "A" is given to the experimental group and the result "B" is observed. The control group is not exposed to "A" and their condition is compared to the experimental group to see what effects "A" might have had in producing "B". In the causal comparative method, the investigator reverses this process, observing a result "B" which already exists and searches back through several possible causes ("A" type of events) that are related to "B".

2. It yields useful information concerning the nature of phenomena: what goes with what, under what conditions, in what sequences and patterns, and the like.
3. Improvements in techniques, statistical methods and designs with partial control features, in recent years, have made these studies more defensible.

Weakness

1. The main weakness of any ex post facto design is the lack of control over independent variables. Within the limits of selection, the investigator must take the facts as he finds them with no opportunity to arrange the conditions or manipulate the variables that influenced the facts in the first place. To reach sound conclusions, the investigator must consider all the other possible reasons or plausible rival hypotheses which might account for the results obtained. To the extent that he can successfully justify his conclusions against these other alternatives, he is in a position of relative strength.
2. The difficulty in being certain that the relevant causative factor is actually included among the many factors under study.
3. The complication that no single factor is the cause of an outcome but some combination and interaction of factors go together under certain conditions to yield a given outcome.
4. A phenomenon may result not only from multiple causes but also from one cause in one instance and from another cause in another instance.
5. When a relationship between two variables is discovered, determining which is the cause and which the effect may be difficult.

6. The fact that two, or more, factors are related does not necessarily imply a cause and effect relationship. They may all simply be related to an additional factor not recognized or observed.
7. Classifying subjects into dichotomous groups (e.g. "Achievers" and "Non-achievers"), for the purpose of comparison is fraught with problems, since categories like these are vague, variable and transitory. Such investigations often do not yield useful findings.
8. Comparative studies in natural situations do not allow controlled selection of subjects. Locating existing groups of subjects are similar in all respects except for their exposure to one variable is extremely difficult.

Steps

1. Define the problem.
2. Survey the literature.
3. State the hypotheses.
4. List the assumptions upon which the hypotheses and procedures will be based.
5. Design the approach.
6. Validate the data gathering techniques.
7. Describe, analyze and interpret the findings in clear, precise terms. (Van Dalen 1979).

True Experimental Research

The purpose of true experimental research is to investigate possible cause and effect relationships by exposing one or more experimental groups to one or more treatment conditions and comparing the results to one or more control groups not receiving the treatment.

Examples

1. To investigate the effects of two methods of teaching a twelfth grade history program as a function of class size (large and small) and levels of student intelligence (high, average, low)

using random assignment of teachers and students by intelligence level to method and class size.

2. To investigate the effects of a new drug abuse prevention program on the attitudes of high school students using experimental and control groups who are either exposed or not exposed to the program, respectively and using a pretest-posttest design in which only half of the students randomly receive the pretest to determine how much of an attitude change can be attributed to pretesting or to the educational program.
3. To investigate the effects of two methods of pupil evaluation on the performance of children in the twenty three elementary schools of a given suburban district. N in this study would be the number of classrooms, rather than children and the method would be assigned by stratified random techniques such that there would be a balanced distribution of the two methods to classrooms across grade levels and socio economic locations of schools.

Characteristics

1. Requires rigorous management of experimental variables and conditions either by direct control/manipulation or through randomization.
2. Typically uses a control group as a baseline against which to compare the group(s) receiving the experimental treatment.
3. Concentrates on the control of variance.
   (a) To maximize the variance of the variable(s) associated with the research hypotheses.

   (b) To minimize the variance of extraneous or "unwanted" variables that might affect the experimental outcomes, but are not themselves the object of study.

   (c) To minimize the error or random variance, including so called errors of measurement.

   Best solution: Random selection of subjects, random assignment of subjects to groups and random assignment of experimental treatments to groups.

4. Internal validity is the sine qua non of research design and the first objective of experimental methodology. It asks the question: did the experimental manipulation in this particular study really make a difference?
5. External validity is the second objective of experimental methodology. It asks the question: How representative are the findings and can the results be generalized to similar circumstances and subjects? (Kerliner, 1973).
6. In classic experimental design, all variables of concern are held constant except a single treatment variable which is deliberately manipulated or allowed to vary. Advances in methodology such as factorial designs and the analysis of variance now allow the experimenter to permit more than one variable to be manipulated or varied concurrently across more than one experimental group.This permits the simultaneous across more than one experimental group. This permits the simultaneous determination of (1) the effects of the principal independent variables (treatments), (2) the variation associated with classificatory variables and (3) the interaction of selected combinations of independent and / or classificatory variables.
7. While the experimental approach is the most powerful because of the control it allows over relevant variables, it is also the most restrictive and artificial. This is a major weakness in applications involving human subjects in real world situations, since human beings often act differently if their behaviour is artificially restricted, manipulated, or exposed to systematic observation and evaluation (Kerliner, 1973).

Seven Steps in Experimental Research

1. Survey the literature relating to the problem.
2. Identify and define the problem.
3. Formulate a problem hypothesis, deducing the consequences and defining basic terms and variables.
4. Construct an experimental plan

(a) Identify all non experimental variables that might contaminate the experiment, and determine how to control them.

(b) Select a research design.

(c) Select a sample of subjects to represent a given population, assign subjects to groups and assign experimental treatments to groups.

(d) Select or construct and validate instruments to measure the outcome of the experiment.

(e) Outline procedures for collecting the data and possibly conduct a pilot or "trial run" test to perfect the instruments or design.

(f) State the statistical or null hypothesis.

5. Conduct the experiments

6. Reduce the raw data in a manner that will produce the best appraisal of the effect which is presumed to exist.

7. Apply an appropriate test of significance to determine the confidence one can place on the results of the study.

Quasi-Experimental Research

The purpose of quasi experiment research is to approximate the conditions of the true experiment in a setting which does not allow the control and or manipulation of all relevant variables. The researcher must clearly understand what compromises exist in the internal and external validity of his design and proceed within these limitations.

Examples

1. To investigate the effects of spaced versus massed practice in the memorizing of vocabulary lists in four high school foreign language classes without being able to assign students to the treatment at random or to supervise closely their practice periods.

2. To assess the effectiveness of three approaches to teaching basic principles and concepts in economics to primary grade children when some of the teachers inadvertently were allowed

to volunteer for one of the approaches because of its impressive looking materials.

3. Educational research involving a pretest posttest design in which such variables as maturation effect of testing, statistical regression, selective attrition and stimulus novelty or adaptation, are unavoidable or overlooked.
4. Most studies of the social problems of delinquency, rioting, smoking or instance of heart disease, where control and manipulation are not always feasible (Donald, 1957).

Characteristics

1. Quasi-experimental research typically involves applied settings where it is not possible to control all the relevant variables but only some of them. The researcher gets as close to the true experimental rigor as conditions allow, carefully qualifying the important exceptions and limitations. Therefore, this research is characterized by methods of partial control based on a careful identification of factors influencing both internal and external validity listed on pages.
2. The distinction between true and quasi-experimental research is tenuous, particularly where human subjects are involved as in education. A careful study of the paradigms presented on will clarify the relative nature of this distinction as a matter of approximation on a continuum between "one shot case studies" of an action research of approximation on a continuum between "one shot case studies" of an action research nature to experimental control group designs with randomization and rigorous management of all foreseeable variables influencing internal and external validity.
3. While action research can have quasi-experimental status, it is often so unformalized as to deserve separate recognition. Once the research plan systematically examines the validity question, moving out of the intuitive and ex-exploratory realm, the beginnings of experimental methodology are visible.

Steps to Quasi-experimental Research: The same as with true experimental research, carefully recognizing each limitation to the internal and external validity of the design. (The term "quasi-experimental" was first introduced into the literature in 1957 by Donald T. Campbell and reiterated in subsequent work with Julian C. Stanley)

Action Research

Purpose

To develop new skills or new approaches and to solve problems with direct application to the classroom or working world setting.

Example

An in-service training program to help train counselors to work more effectively with minority group children; to develop an exploratory program in appropriate rural technology course to solve the problem of apathy in a required agricultural "orientation" to test a fresh approach to interesting more students in taking vocational education courses.

Characteristics

1. Practical and directly relevant to an actual situation in the working world. The subjects are the classroom students, the staff, or others with whom you are primarily involved.
2. Provides an orderly frame work for problem solving and new developments that is superior to the impressionistic, fragmentary approach that otherwise typifies developments in education. It also is empirical in the sense that it relies on actual observations and behavioural data and does not fall back on subjective committee "studies" or opinions of people based on their past experience.
3. Flexible and adaptive, allowing changes during the trial period and sacrificing control in favour of responsiveness and on the spot experimentation and innovation.
4. While attempting to be systematic, action research lack scientific rigor because its internal and external validity is weak. Its objective is situational, its sample is restricted and unrepresentative, and it has little control over independent variables. Hence, its findings, while useful within the practical

dimension of the situation, do not directly contribute to the general body of educational knowledge.

Steps

1. Define the problem or set the goal. What is it that needs improvement or that might be developed as a new skill or solution?
2. Review the literature to learn whether others have met similar problems or achieved related objectives.
3. Formulate testable hypotheses or strategies of approach, stating them in clear, specific, pragmatic language.
4. Arrange the research setting and spell out the procedures and conditions. What are the particular things you will do in an attempt to meet your objectives?
5. Establish evaluation criteria, measurement techniques and other means of acquiring useful feedback.
6. Analyze the data and evaluate the outcomes (Michael, 1982).

Purpose

To reconstruct the past systematically and objectively by collecting, evaluating, verifying and synthesizing evidence to establish facts and reach defensible conclusions, often in relation to particular hypotheses.

Research Methods Versus Research Methodology

It seems appropriate at this juncture to explain the difference between research methods and research methodology. Research methods may be understood as all those methods of research that deal with the purpose of the study, the nature of the problem, and the alternatives appropriate for their investigation. Once the purpose has been specified, the study should have explicit scope and direction, and attention can be focused on a delimited target area. The nature of the problem then plays the major role in determining what approaches are suitable.

Methodology

Methodology is the procedure of research techniques. It is the logic of scientific investigation. It is not a research model employed in a particular project but is a technique which entails theoretical principles as well as a framework that provides guidelines about how research is done in the context of a particular paradigm. It translates the principles of a paradigm into research language and shows how the society can be explained and studied.

Literally, 'methodology' means the science of methods. It contains the standards and principles employed to guide the choice, structure, process and use of methods, as directed by the underlying paradigm. Methodology in sociology includes: (i) the analysis of the basic assumptions of science in general and of sociology in particular, (ii) the process of theory construction, (iii) the interrelationship of theory and research, and (iv) the procedures of empirical investigation. Thus, methodology is not concerned with building knowledge but deals with the procedures conceptual, logical and research by which knowledge is built. Methodology is determined not by the research model but rather by the principles of research entailed in the paradigm. The methodology may either be qualitative or quantitative. (Ahuja, 2003).

Method

Method is a tool or an instrument employed to gather empirical evidence and to analyze data. It is building of scientific knowledge. In scientific method, knowledge is built through observation, experimentation, generalization and verification. The scientific method is based on the assumption that knowledge is based on what is experienced through the senses and that the statement is to be accepted as true and meaningful if it is empirically verifiable.

Accordingly to Sarandakos (1998:34), although methods in general are methodological, their content, structure and process are dictated by the underlying methodology. For instance, observation as a method (of data collection) is used both in qualitative and quantitative studies but participant observation is more used in qualitative studies while non participant observation is employed in quantitative studies. Similarly, in interview method, unstructured interview is used more in qualitative studies and structured interview in quantitative studies.

Methods are not used for determining the type of methodology without considering factors relating to its purpose, process, type of analysis and other factors.

Table 1.2

Distinctions between Research Methods and Research Methodology

	Methods	*Methodology*
1.	A scientific method is a systematic study of a limited and definite subject matter.	Methodology is the actual procedure of collecting and ordering the data e.g., questionnaire, schedule or interview in social research.
2.	Methods are definite:Every method has a fixed outlay and follows scheduled steps.	Methodology keeps changing. e.g. In modern social research, taking down of notes has been replaced by the use of tape recorder and naked eye observation is giving way to photo and movie camera.
3.	Method is common to all sciences: A scientific method is common to every science. It has five phases: observation noting, classification, generalization and verification. In every science the same order is followed.	Methodology is not common to all sciences: Unlike methods, techniques are not common to all sciences. In no science except social research, the use of mailed questionnaire is made. It can obviously have no value for physical sciences; the techniques of micro analysis and telescopic observation have no place in social research.
4.	Method is underived.	Methodology is derived.

	Method is independent of techniques.	Techniques are dependent upon the method. For instance, the various techniques of observation follow from the fact that observation is part of the scientific method. The researcher may observe through the naked eye, or with the help of any other helping aid.
5.	Aim of the method is wider and dominant:The aim of a scientific method is systematic knowledge of a certain subject matter. The aim of the method is wider and dominant and includes within it the aim of the techniques.	Aim of the Methodology is limited and subservient: The aim of the Methodology is merely collection and ordering of facts.The technique's aim is limited and subservient to that of methods.
6.	The Different kinds of methods used are :- The main scientific methods are (a) induction (b) deduction (c) comparison (d) historical (e) structural and (f) functional.	Different kinds of Methodologies are :- The main techniques of social research are: (a) observation (b) Questionnaire (c) schedule and interview (d) documentary study etc.

Source: Saravanavel, 1999.

Research Methodology is a way to systematically solve the research problem. It may be understood as a science of studying how research is done scientifically and study the various steps that are generally adopted by a researcher in analyzing his research problem along with the logic behind them. It is necessary for the researcher to know not only the research methods / but also the methodology, pertaining to his particular research. Broadly it will include the sampling methods, observational method, statistical method and operational method.

Researchers not only need to know how to develop certain indices or tests, how to calculate the mean, the mode, the median or the standard deviation or chi – square, how to apply particular research techniques, but they also need to know which of these methods or techniques, are relevant and which are not, and what would they mean and indicate and why. Researchers also need to understand the assumptions underlying various techniques and they need to know the criteria by which they can decide, that certain techniques and procedures will be applicable to certain problems and others will not. All this means that it is necessary for the researchers to design his methodology for his problem as the same may differ from problem to problem. For example, an architect, who designs a building, has to consciously evaluate the basis of his decision i.e., he has to evaluate why and on what basis he selects a particular size, number and location of doors, windows and ventilators, uses particular materials and not others and the like. Similarly, in research the scientist has to expose the research decisions to evaluation before they are implemented. He has to specify very clearly and precisely on what decisions he selects them so that they can be evaluated by others also.

From what has been stated it can be derived that research methodology has many dimensions and research methods do constitute a part of the Research methodology. The scope of research methodology is wider than that of research methods. Thus, when a researcher deals with a research methodology he does not only talk of the research methods but also consider the logic behind the methods he uses in the context of research study and explain why he is using a particular method or technique and why he is not using others so that research results are capables of being evaluated by the researcher himself or by others. Why a research study has been undertaken, how the research problem has been defined, in what way and why the hypothesis has been formulated, what data have been collected and what particular method has been adopted, why particular technique of analyzing data has been used and a host of similar other questions are usually answered when research methodology is discussed concerning a problem or study.

Table 1.3

Distinction between Basic Research and Applied Research

Pure (Behavioural) Research	*Applied (Behavioural) Research*
1. Aims to contribute to theory and techniques of the discipline.	Aims to solve or ameliorate a problem.
2. Studies any problem.	Studies problems with important social consequences.
3. Studies a problem usually from the focus of one discipline.	Often several disciplines collaborate for solving the problem.
4. Restricts to research.	Often it is solved in action or administration, not only in research.
5. Requires mainly technical judgment.	Requires a sense of what the situation and personalities can bear.
6. Seeks generalization.	Often studies individual cases without the objective to generalize.
7. Accepts the hypothesis that variables not measured remain constant.	Recognize that other variables are constantly changing.
8. Looks for the basic processes.	Looks for any variable which makes the desired difference.
9. Content with small differences if statistically significant.	Interested in important differences.
10. Tries to say why things happen.	Tries to say how things can be changed.
11. Attempts to get all the facts.	Should attempt only to correct facts which speak reasonably directly to practitioner decisions,

	to actionable alternatives recognized in advance.
12. Aims at publishing a research report (on the average this can be done about five years after the field work is done).	Aims at bringing about actionable points quickly in a series of memoranda and discussions with practitioners.
13. Reports in technical language of the discipline.	Reports in common language.

Source: Saravanavel, 1999.

Qualitative Research, Quantitative Research and Mixed Research

Pure quantitative research relies on the collection of quantitative data (i.e., numerical data) and follows the other characteristics of the quantitative research paradigm, a qualitative research relies on the collection of qualitative data (i.e., non-numerical data such as words and pictures) and follows the other characteristics of the qualitative research paradigm. Mixed research involves the mixing of quantitative and qualitative research methods, approaches or paradigms. The exact mixture that is considered appropriate will depend on the research questions and the situation and practical issues facing a researcher. All three research approaches can provide insights with which one attempts to solve the problems facing researchers. The following are the key differences between the three research approaches. First, the quantitative research approach focuses on the deductive component of the scientific method because the focus is generally on hypothesis testing and theory testing. Quantitative research is said to be confirmatory because researchers test or attempt to confirm their hypotheses. On the other hand, qualitative research relies more on the inductive component of the scientific method and is used to come up with or generate new hypotheses and theories. Qualitative research is often exploratory, that is, it is often used when little is known about a certain topic or when an inductive approach is deemed more appropriate to learn more about a topic.

Most researchers probably take a mixed approach to the inductive-deductive distinction because at some point in the research process, most researchers will use both induction and deduction. Scientific reasoning is a cyclical process of induction and deduction. In quantitative research, hypotheses are typically deduced from a theory or currently available explanations and the predicted observable outcomes are deduced from the hypotheses. Data are then collected to determine whether the hypotheses and as a result the theory or explanation, are supported. However, it is common for unanticipated outcomes to appear in quantitative research findings. When this happens, quantitative researchers commonly enter the inductive mode of generating new or revised hypotheses and explanations, which will be put to the test during a future research study. Likewise, in qualitative research, after inductive hypotheses and a tentative theory have been generated from initial observations, the observable consequences of these are often deduced and then tested through additional observations. In short, stating that quantitative researchers follow the deductive method and qualitative researchers follow the inductive methods is really a matter of emphasis, not exclusion. Mixed researchers explicitly state that they use both induction and deduction.

Quantitative and qualitative research is also distinguished by different views of human behavior. It is generally assumed in quantitative research that behaviour is highly predictable. The assumption of determinism was traditionally made, which means that all events have a cause.

Table – 1.4

Emphasis of Quantitative, Mixed and Qualitative Research

	Quantitative Research	*Mixed Research*	*Qualitative Research*
Scientific method	Deductive or "top-down" The researcher tests hypotheses and theory with data	Deductive and inductive	Inductive or "bottomup" The researcher generates new hypotheses and grounded theory from data collected during field work.

View of human behaviour	Behavior is regular and predictable	Behaviour is some what predictable	Behaviour is fluid, dynamic, situational, social, contextual and personal.
Most common research objectives	Description, explanation and prediction	Multiple objectives	Description, exploration and discovery.
Focus	Narrow-angle lens, testing specific hypotheses	Multi-lens focus	Wide-angle and "deep-angle" lens, examining the breadth and depth of phenomena to learn more about them.
Nature of Observa--tion	Attempt to study behavior under controlled conditions	Study behavior in more than one context or condition	Study behaviour in natural environments, study the context in which behavior occurs.
Nature of reality	Objective	Commonsense realism and pragmatic view of world (i.e., what works is, what is "real" or true)	Subjective, personal and socially constructed.
Form of data collected	Collect quantitative data based on precise measurement using structured and validated data collection instruments (e.g., closed ended items, rating scales, behavioural responses)	Multiple forms	Collect qualitative data (e.g., in-depth interviews, participant observation, field notes and open-ended questions) The researcher is the primary data collection instrument.

Nature of data	Variables	Mixture of variables, words and images	Words, images, categories
Data analysis	Identify statistical relationships	Quantitative and qualitative	Search for patterns, themes and holistic features
Results	Generalizable findings	Corroborated findings may generalize	Particularistic findings, Representation of insider (i.e.,"emic") view point, Present multiple perspectives.
Form of final report	Statistical report (e.g., with correlations, comparisons of means and reporting of statistical significance of findings)	Electric and pragmatic	Narrative report with contextual description and direct quotations from research participants.

Source: Monash University Ph.D., Research Guidelines, 2009.

For example, the process by which children learn to read is determined by one or more causes. Likewise, there are causes for adolescents dropping out of school. Because quantitative research has not identified any unerring laws of human behavior, most contemporary quantitative researchers search for probabilistic causes. A probabilistic statement might go like this: "Adolescents who become involved with drugs and alcohol are more likely to drop out of high school than are adolescents who do not become involved with drugs and alcohol." The point is that most quantitative researchers try to identify cause-and-effect relationships that enable them to make probabilistic predictions and generalizations. On the other hand, qualitative researchers often focus on the fluid and dynamic dimensions of behaviour. Behaviour is seen to be more situational and context bound than generalizable. Different groups are said to construct different realities or perspectives and the focus is on how patterns of behavior vary from group to group and from situation to situation.

These views about human behavior are not set in storne, however, for example, when taking a mixed mode approach, quantitative researchers might study the influence of context and the dynamic process of behaviour (e.g., social psychologists examine individuals as they interact and change their behaviours in social situations). Quantitative research also focuses on how results vary according to the characteristics of the participants. Similarly, when taking a mixed mode approach, qualitative researchers often try to develop explanations of behaviour (theories) that sometimes include causal language and they attempt to make generalizations. In short, many researchers operate in either the quantitative or the qualitative mode, cross over into the mixed research mode.

Current Trends in Research

The 21st century society is known as a "Knowledge Society." Education just like the other educational systems has been based far too much on purely transferring knowledge or building knowledge capital. What is essential is to know how to "manage knowledge". When academic knowledge is integrated into realities academicians learn how to apply all that they learn to build a better world. To meet the challenges four pillars of education and research are advocated by UNESCO.

1. Learning to know or capacity to absorb new knowledge, whether the young persons' minds are being trained so that throughout their lives they can continue to absorb the exploding knowledge that doubles every five years.
2. Learning to do means that the knowledge imparted to young people should also make them capable of gainful employment so that they become productive members of the society.
3. Learning to live together, that is, education does need to encompass the necessity for young people to become positive and integrated elements of their respective societies.
4. Learning to be, that is, education must contribute to the all

round development of each individual's mind and body, intelligence, sensibility, aesthetic sense, personal responsibility and spiritual values. The holistic education must acknowledge the multiple dimensions of the human personality: physical, intellectual, aesthetic, emotional and spiritual thus moving towards the perennial dream of an integrated individual living on the harmonious planet.

In the development of knowledge two things are happening simultaneously, one micro specializations; the other, integration and interrelationship between different disciplines. Such a scenario demands creation of institutions focusing not only on specialized fields but providing research in multidisciplinary fields. Knowledge is developing most rapidly at the intersection of disciplines. Integration takes us away from too much specialization that many times proves to be ineffective. The profile of the learners that will fit into the 21st century, as outlined by Christopher Ball whose educational work has placed great importance on the benefits of society giving enough attention and resource, to the developmental needs of the learners has become highly significant. He envisions the future learners to be flexible generalists rather than specialists. The flexible generalists are persons equipped with necessary levels of knowledge, skills and values to adjust readily to multiple career challenges and make through their own personal development a significant contribution to the life of the country and the world at large.

Integrated or Trans-disciplinary Research creates new opportunities for design research to become multi-disciplinary and this, in turn, creates novel possibilities for better interdisciplinary research communication and innovative research outcomes. When one shifts outside the parameters established by accepted research paradigms and academically constructed disciplines one starts to work trans-disciplinary. The determinants of a potential solution involve the integration of different skills in a frame work of action. This provides the researcher with the opportunity to be creative, by making use of the methods best suited to get the proper process covered and the results reflected. In the design disciplines this brings together the processes of innovation, visualization and imagination. Communication plays an important role in integrated research. The communication between the researcher and the community leads to new research configurations and combinations. The key factor in this type of research method used is based on stimulating, initiating and facilitating communication.

It is evident that integrated research requires a new approach to research. With an increasing number of research participants and variety in research topics, single institution systems are often unable to accommodate research requests. Instead facilitating a research system, based on centre-to centre research, to accommodate and broaden the scope of research is the need for the day.

In this context: to quote an example. Metcalf's law states that the 'value' or 'power' of a network increases in proportion to the square of the number of network. In other words, if one has four nodes on a network, its 'value' would be four squared 4^2 or 16.

Metcalfe's Law

Metcalfe's law states that the value of a telecommunications network is proportional to the square of the number of users of the system (n^2). First formulated by Robert Metcalfe in regard to internet, Metcalfe's law explains many of the network effects of communication technologies and networks such as the Internet, social networking and the World Wide Web. It is related to the fact that the number of unique connections in a network of a number of nodes (n) can be expressed mathematically as $n(n-1)/2$, which follows n^2 asymptotically.

The law has often been illustrated using the example of fax machines: a single fax machine is useless, but the value of every fax machine increases with the total number of fax machines in the network, because the total number of people with whom each user may send and receive documents increases.

In fact, Metcalfe's law measures the potential number of contacts, i.e., the technological side of a network. However the social utility of a network depends upon the number of nodes in contact. For instance, if Indian and Non- Indian users don't understand each other, the utility of a network of users that speak the other language is at zero, and the law has to be calculated for the two networks separately.

Robert Metcalfe's law states that the "value" or "Power" of a network increases in proportion to the square of the number of nodes on the network.

Marc Andresen, one of the founders of the web, said:

A network in general behaves in such a way that the more nodes that are added to it, the whole thing gets more valuable for everyone on it because all of a sudden there's all this new stuff that wasn't there before. You saw it with the phone system. The more phones that are on the network, the more valuable it is to everyone because then you can call these people. Federal Express, in order to grow their business, would add a node in Topeka and business in New York would spike. You see it on the Internet all the time. Every new node, every new server, every new user expand the possibilities for everyone else who's already there.

More recently, David Weinberg, writing in his 'Small pieces loosely joined': a unified theory of the web (Perseus, 2002), pointed to Reed's Law, a refinement of Metcalf's Law. Weinberg pointed out that Metcalf's Law was formulated in an era of one-to-one communications (e.g. telephone network), but in this day of virtual communities and group communications, there are exponentially more ways in which to create network connections.

1. http://en.wikipedia.org/wiki/matcalf's law
2. http://www.ec.njit.edu/urobertoso/infosci/metcalf.html

Inter–Disciplinary Research

Human relationships have multiple aspects such as economic, social, political, cultural, religious, psychological, anthropological, etc., from a particular view point. Beside the view point, each discipline has a method peculiar to it, which distinguishes it from other disciplines. Some social problems are such that they are connected with two or more aspects. In other words, different aspects of these social problems may be studied in different fields of study. The study of such problems, therefore, requires the use of methods peculiar to several approaches. This is known as interdisciplinary approach. In this approach the methods peculiar to several disciplines are utilized to study a particular problem.

Main Reasons for the Need of Inter-disciplinary Approach

1. **Mutual Relationships of Different Disciplines**: Though each discipline is considered as distinct, most of the disciplines are interconnected. Therefore, studies and researches in one discipline are bound to influence other disciplines. Hence, the need of inter – disciplinary approach is obvious. e.g., while writing a descriptive grammar for a tribal language one has to integrate anthropology, linguistics, culture, economics, geography, history and so on.
2. **Imperfection of a Single Discipline / Approach**: No discipline is complete or perfect in itself. For example, economics cannot solve all the social problems nor can medicine relieve all the tensions. Each social science is concerned only with a limited aspect of society. Therefore, in order to study the total society one will have to take recourse of several disciplines. Therefore, the interdisciplinary approach is utilized.
3. **Several Aspects of Social Phenomenon**: Social phenomena are complex. Each social phenomenon has several aspects. The physical, economic, religious, social, cultural, political, psychological and other factors influence social phenomena. No social phenomenon can be completely free from external influences. In such a situation, in order to know the social phenomenon, it is necessary to find other factors determining them. To know all these factors lying in the fields of different disciplines, an interdisciplinary approach is required.
4. **Need of Objectives**: The need to increase objectivity requires that the same problem should be studied from different aspects or angles. Thus, in order to make research more objective and successful, an inter-disciplinary approach is required.

Types of Inter–disciplinary Approach

Inter–disciplinary approach is used in various ways. The form of methods changes when it is used. As a general rule, the following types of inter–disciplinary approach are more prevalent these days:

1. In inter – disciplinary approach various sciences are coordinated. This type is such that the investigator himself conducts research and seeks help from other experts wherever required. Necessary help is secured in the form of expert advice from the researchers of other sciences. Sometimes the help is secured from other fields of study as well.
2. In a different type of inter – disciplinary approach, different experts of different disciplines conduct researches in their own field. They study a problem independently and themselves prepare a plan of study in their own field. However, they meet from time to time and hold discussions. In the end, all of them send reports of their studies to the central office where all these reports are coordinated to arrive at some interdisciplinary approach.
3. Thirdly, the investigators from different disciplines work in collaboration right from the beginning to the end. They work as members of a research group or team in which the functions are divided and every member is responsible to fulfill his/ her own function.

Advantages of Inter – Disciplinary Approach

1. **Integral Study**: The study of a problem in a particular discipline and through a particular method is generally one sided and limited. The integral approach, on the other hand, leads to an integral and total study. Thus, it is particularly useful for a deep and all round study of a problem.
2. **Elimination of Errors**: If the same problem is simultaneously studied in several disciplines using different approaches, the possibility of errors diminishes. Firstly, it attempts to study all the aspects and secondly, the problem is studied in several disciplines. This makes interdisciplinary approach very much advantageous.
3. **Objectivity**: Every researcher has his own prejudices, which retard the objectivity of his study. In interdisciplinary approach, several researchers as a team, who considerably diminish and eliminate the influence of their personal prejudices, increase objectivity of research thereby.

4. **Goodwill among Different Disciplines**: When several experts work as members of a team, they come to realize the importance of other disciplines. Therefore, interdisciplinary approach creates goodwill among the fields of different disciplines.

Disadvantages of Inter–disciplinary Approach

In spite of the above mentioned advantages, the interdisciplinary approach sufferers from several disadvantages:

1. **Limited utility**: The inter–disciplinary approach is useful only in the study of some general and practical problems. It is not utilized in the study of complex and theoretical problems. Therefore, its utility is limited.
2. **Less Organized and Systematic**: The study organized on the basis of inter– disciplinary approach is generally less organized and systematic than expected, so much so that sometimes the study becomes entirely out of control.
3. **More Expensive**: As this approach of study requires the services of several experts coming from different fields, it requires much more expenditure as compared to other methods.
4. **Unreliable Conclusions**: As the function of coordination is mostly done by one or more senior researchers their prejudices and sense of superiority may become hindrances in the proper coordination of results. Therefore, the conclusions reached by interdisciplinary approach are sometimes not reliable. (Lal 2002).

2

RESEARCH PROCESS

Research having its origin in science, is oriented towards the development of theories and its most familiar paradigm is the experimental method, in which hypothesis are logically derived from the theory and put to test under controled conditions. Research has brought new areas of knowledge both in theory and applied aspects of education. Research could be classified as pure, basic or theoretical research and applied research. Pure research is concerned only with the development of knowledge. However, applied research is practical oriented. Research is not just a casual observation but a systematic approach adopting particular methods and procedures. Scientific aptitude, correct perception and testing the data for their validity are emphasized in research. Research will help one to prove, disprove or improve his hypothesis. Research programs have the following basic processes or steps to follow.

Steps in Research Process

1. Statement of the Problem/Formulation of Research Problem/ Choice of the subject.
2. Review of Source Material / Survey of Related Literature.
3. Introduction, Definition (or Explication) of Concepts, Objectives
4. Identification (or Listing of Variables).
5. Formulation of Hypothesis / Statements of Hypothesis.
6. Definition of Universe (or population), Selection of Sample.
7. Preparation of Study Design/Designing the Methods of Data Collection/Research
8. Design.

9. Data Collection and Processing.
10. Analysis and Interpretation - Evaluation
11. Findings obtained and Conclusion
12. Bibliography

Fig. 2.1

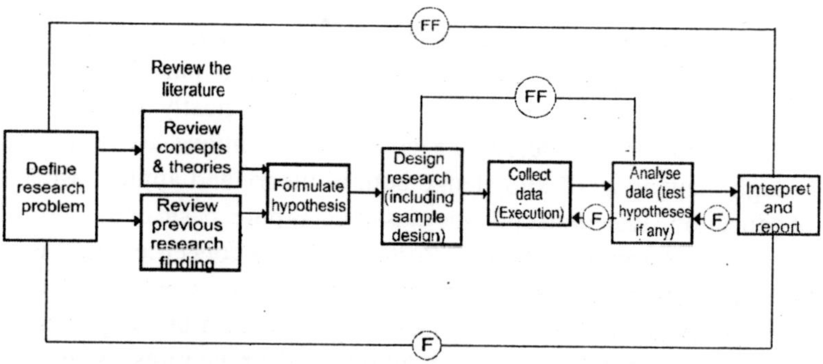

Research process consists of a series of actions or steps necessary to effectively carry out research and the desired sequencing these steps.The chart shown in Fig. 2.1 illustrates a research process (Kothari, 2009).

The chart indicates that the research process consists of a number of closely related activities, as shown through I to VII. But such activities overlap continuously rather than following a strictly prescribed sequence. At times, the first step determines the nature of the last step to be undertaken. If subsequent procedures have not been taken into account in the early stages, serious difficulties may arise which may even prevent the completion of the study. One should remember that the various steps involved in a research process are not mutually exclusive; nor are they separate and distinct. They do not necessarily follow each other in any specific order and the researcher has to be constantly anticipating at each step in the research process the requirements of the subsequent steps. However, the following order concerning various steps provides a useful procedural guideline regarding the research process: (1) formulating the research problem; (2) extensive literature survey; (3) developing the hypothesis; (4)

preparing the research design; (5) determining sample design; (6) collecting data; (7) execution of the project; (8) analysis of data; (9) hypothesis testing; (10) generalization and interpretation, and (11) preparation of the report or presentation of the results i.e., formal write up of conclusion is reached.

Statement of the Problem / Choice of the Subject

Selection of Research Topic

The Selection of Research problem firstly depends on whether research is being conducted as a requirement of a degree or is it for academic interests. If the research is only to fulfill some requirements for obtaining a degree, the problem may be more specific and limited in scope and may offer itself for completion within a specified time. If the researcher fails to select such a problem as would be completed in a reasonable amount of time, he would often run into difficulties and may go without the desired degree. On the other hand, if the research is of academic interest, time should not be a binding factor. Many a time the entire lifetime of a researcher goes towards exploring something new through his research efforts. He does not want any research degree but only does the research with the sole objective of enriching his personal knowledge as well as that of the general academic world.

The selection of the problem as a requirement for degree further depends on the level of research of learning. Many times research problems are selected at M.A., M. Th., / M. Phil., Ph.D., levels. But it is obvious that the levels of learning at these stages are different and therefore, demand different treatments to research problems.

Not only is the selection of problem important but its statement is also equally important. If the problem is not carefully and scientifically stated, it may lead to confusion regarding the specific interest for which the research investigation has been undertaken.
1. One should choose a definite and specific subject of interest and value within the limits of one's time. He should be able to procure the necessary materials. It is better not to choose a subject which will involve technical information beyond one's comprehension. The topic should be framed in a declarative and unbiased way. It may be defined

as to get an idea and to express the problem in some reasonably manageable way (Sadhu, & Amarjit, 1980).

Statement of the Problem

Statement of the problem including, limitations of time period, books to be examined and the field work with a particular people are to be stated immediately following the statement of the problem and some elaboration should be given e.g., In what ways the proposed research does in fact focus upon? What can be regarded as a problem? Is there a social problem such as regarding the oppressed people? What are the major dimensions of the problem? There must be an indication – why the problem has been chosen? What led the researcher to choose a particular problem?

Other Things to Consider

If there has been previous research done on the same problem in some cases, proposed research must go beyond the previous research. The researcher must indicate how he is going to investigate the problem. One must be sure of his or her main perspective. If it is social history, it must be indicated whether it is a survey, a case study or ethnography. The sources of data should be indicated. If some one is writing the concept of a leader, his writings will become as the primary sources, along with a selection of what have so far been found as major secondary sources. Visiting of libraries, places, interviews must be mentioned. In gathering of data and tools a brief description should also be given such as – where the data and tools are to be secured, and how they will be developed and how the resultant data will be analyzed. Time limit must be mentioned; e.g., the total time period.

There should be a tentative outline to go with, after the approval of the thesis committee and it could be modified later. The bibliography of selected books and other materials should be mentioned. The research proposal should be viewed as a plan for investigating a problem. It should reflect rigorous conceptualization of what is perceived to be the problem and how the problem will be investigated. It involves, writer's motive, interest, time and effort. The research person should not choose a topic in haste. The topic of choice must be of one's own interest and after much contemplation, planning and finding of available sources, he or she should choose the topic. A topic could be the choice of the researcher after consulting the guide mentor for constructive guidelines for proper choice. The research guide can help the researcher fellow to choose his topic, knowing his interest and desire.

Formulating a Research Problem

A Research problem, in general refers to some difficulty which a researcher experiences in the context of either a theoretical or practical situation and wants to obtain a solution for the same (Kothari, 1999). A statement of a problem is a clear and concise statement, preferably of only of few sentences in a nutshell, which specify the precise problem or question for which an answer is to be sought in the research undertaking. The purpose of research is to find a solution to the specific problem or question. The statement of the problem should therefore be not only clear and precise; it should also present a manageable problem–a problem for which the necessary research can be carried out with in the time and other resources available to the researcher. The proposed title for the anticipated research should be clearly stated precisely and the title should delineate the area of investigation. A sub title may be included which helps to state the subject area more precisely.

Recognition of Problems

This may indicate even the needs in a person's society. e.g., what is the root cause of continued poverty? How can the weaker sections secure greater access to health care and education? What can be done to protect the forests and sources of safe drinking water? Those are general questions but they direct attention to problems and needs among the people, and cry for solutions (Mabry, 1999).

Components of a Research Problem

The faculty to formulate a simple worded problem can be developed through the phrasing technique. The formation of a problem depends to a large extent upon the knowledge of the components of a problem. A researcher should identify five components of a problem.

1. Individual or group has the problem:

2. The researcher must have some objectives, goals, ends or desires.
3. The researcher must have alternatives to achieve ends and objectives.
4. He should have more than one alternative course of action for better achievement with efficiency.
5. There must be one or more environments to which the problem pertains. The discovery of a problem is the first precondition in the formulation of a research, (Saravanavel, 1999).

Sources of Research Problem

The following sources could help to select the research problem:

1. Theory of one's own interest.
2. Daily problems.
3. Technological changes.
4. Unexplored areas.
5. Discussions with experts and authorities including the supervisor or research advisor.

Choice of a problem for investigation could be based on a given theory and the interest of the research person. Everyday problems constantly present something new and worthy of investigation and it depends on the sharpness of the researcher's intellect to knit his daily experiences into a research problem.

Evaluating the Problem

If the problem rejected could be a good one the answers are affirmative for the following questions:

1. Whether the research can solve the problem to have relevant data enough to test the theory.
2. Whether the problem is significant? Whether it has important principle?
3. Whether the problem is a new one? Whether answers are already available?

4. Whether the researche problem is feasible to the researcher?

e.g: The researcher must be able to carry out the study. He must be sure of the data, financial resources, equipment, printing test materials, travel, clerical help, and the time for doing the above research, the courage, determination and aggressiveness in doing the research work.

Review of Source Materials / Survey of Related Literature

Reading the related works provide the necessary knowledge or insight in the area of research interest whether to hypothesis or to gain effective information. A researcher should not confine himself to studies that are immediately relevant to the area of interest. He has to study about the working concepts and theories developed in different research contexts. The researcher has to account for all referred literature in his study. It deals with a literature survey of the existing volumes of similar or related subjects.This helps in understanding the nature and design of the research investigation and provides evidence that the researcher is familiar with what is already known. Since effective research is based upon past knowledge, a survey of the past literature will help to eliminate the duplication of what has been done and sometimes provides clues to formulate useful hypothesis.

Definition (or Explication) of Concepts, Objectives

Definitions of Concept

Technical terms, concepts and specialized words must be defined clearly, e.g., church. "If the term 'church' is the key category for the proposed investigation, will it be used to mean a local body of believers, an organized denomination, the universal body of Christians, past and present or in some other sense?".

Concepts constitute the definitions of what are to be observed. They guide the collection and analysis of data in research. They define the characteristics of the data to be collected. The concepts can be defined in formal manner or in an operational manner. If the researcher simply produces the definition given in a dictionary or glossary for a concept, it is formal (or normal definition). If the researcher attempts to define concepts in terms of all the operational aspects involved therein, it is operational definition. The latter is preferred because it makes the concept precise, clear and comprehensive.

Limitations

The scope of the problem should be clearly indicated with its limitations, e.g., *An investigation of environmental hazards of disposable plastics by tourists in Bangalore*. It could be limited to the impact of environment during a specific period.

Objectives

Objectives are framed in the light of the available resources and the purpose of the study. The objectives are followed by variables, hypotheses, the methods of data collection, which in turn depend on the cost, time and labor. Then the universe and the sample are decided.

Identification or Listing of Variables

The relevant factors that constitute or affect the problem under study are called "variables". There are three types of variables:

1. Independent variables are independent of the outcome itself. They are presumed to cause, effect, or influence the outcome.
2. Dependent variables are dependent on the independent variables. The outcome presumably depends on how these input variables are managed or manipulated.
3. Control variables need to be controlled, held constant or randomized so that their effects are neutralized, cancelled out or equated for all conditions e.g., age, sex, I.Q. socio-economic status, educational level, etc. (Isaac & Michael, 1982)

Formulation of Hypothesis / Statement of Hypothesis

Hypothesis is an assertion that the investigator seeks to investigate. Goode and Hatt have defined it as "A proposition which can be put to test to determine validity. A hypothesis looks forward. It may seem contrary to or in accord with, common sense. It may prove to be correct or incorrect. In any event however, it leads to an empirical test" (Goode & Hatt, 1952).

The formulation of the hypothesis is the central step in good research. Therefore, it is important to give it a great deal of thought. In the absence of a proper or suitable hypothesis, a lot of time and labour of the researcher will be wasted in fruitless research. "Formulation of the hypothesis gives definite point to the inquiry, aids in establishing direction in which to proceed and helps to delimit the field of enquiry by singling and the pertinent facts on which to concentrate and by determining which facts should be set aside, at least for the time being." "The use of hypothesis, thus prevents the researcher from indiscriminate gathering of data which may later prove irrelevant to the problem under study. The formulation of hypothesis thus is very crucial and success or the failure of a research study depends upon how best it has been formulated by the researcher." (Goode & Hatt 1952)

Qualities of a Workable Hypothesis

(a) The Hypothesis should be conceptually clear

To have a clear conception of a hypothesis two things are a must. One, the concepts should be clearly defined. Two, the definitions which are used should be those which are commonly accepted and communicable by the fellow researchers to ensure if it carries the exact sense.

(b) The Hypothesis should be specific

The hypothesis should not be vague or ambitiously formulated. It must be specific, rigid and reasonable in its context and form.

(c) Capable of empirical test

The hypothesis should be such as can be put to empirical test.

(d) Related to a body of theory

It is desirable that the hypothesis selected should be in continuation of any theory already evolved.

(e) Related to available techniques

Whatever hypothesis has been formulated should have an available technique for its testing "the theorists who does not know what techniques are available to test his hypothesis is in a poor way to formulate usable questions"

Selection of Sample/Definition of Universe or Population

Sampling

The primary purpose of research is to discover principles that have universal application. Research therefore, needs adequate and accurate data for this purpose. In order to obtain these data, a researcher conducts investigations into his given population. Information thus can be often derived quickly and cheaply and with significant accuracy from a sample of the total sampling, refers to the investigation of a part of the whole population or universe. A sampling procedure is a technique of selecting a sample from a given population. The important considerations in selecting a sample are to see that it is closely representative of the universe. "The actual selection of a sample should be so done that every item in the universe under consideration must have the same chance of inclusion in the sample." (Young, 1961)

Sampling Techniques

There are a number of sampling techniques for data collection. Important techniques are:

1. Simple Random Sampling.
2. Systematic Sampling.
3. Sampling with probability proportional to size.
4. Stratified Random Sampling.
5. Sub-Sampling, Multi – Stage Sampling.
6. Cluster Sampling.

Preparation of Research Design/ Designing the Methods of Data Collection

Research Design: The formulation of the research design is the selection of an appropriate methodology. The part of the research design outlines the entire research plan. "It describes just what must be done, how it will be done, what data will be needed, what data gathering devices will be employed, how sources of data will be selected, and how the data will be analyzed and conclusion reached."

Selection of proper research methodology is a very crucial problem. If a wrong methodology has been adopted, the results are bound to be vague, implausible and unscientific.The methodology for any research study is drawn in a careful examination of the available literature and depending on a large extent to the imagination and long term vision and understanding of the methodology. It should also include the recent developments in that particular branch of knowledge.

The researcher should state who the subject will be, how they will be selected, the condition under which the data will be collected, what measuring instruments or data gathering techniques will be used and how the data will be analyzed and interpreted. "A research design is the arrangement of condition for collection and analysis of data in a manner that aims to combine relevance to the research with economy in procedure." Generally, research design may vary depending on the researchers' knowledge, skill and resources. Research design is helpful mainly for answering the research questions as validly, objectively, accurately and economically.

Research Design can be organized into nine functional categories based on the differing problem characteristics. (Isaac & Michael, 1982)

1. Historical 2. Descriptive 3. Developmental
4. Case or Field 5. Correlation 6. Casual – Comparative
7. True Experimental 8. Quasi – experimental 9. Action.

Pilot Study

1. Pilot study will permit a preliminary testing of the hypothesis that leads to testing of more precise hypothesis in the main study. It may lead to change some hypotheses, drop some, and bring in new ones.
2. It often provides the research worker with ideas, approaches and clues not foreseen prior to the pilot study.
3. It helps to make the needed alterations that may be useful in the data collecting methods.
4. It greatly reduces the number of treatment errors, because unforeseen problems revealed in the pilot study may be

overcome in redesigning the main study.

5. It may save the research worker from a major expenditure of time and money on a research project that might yield nothing. The pilot study usually provides enough data for the research worker to make a sound decision on the advisability of going ahead with the main study.
6. In the pilot study, the researcher may try out a number of alternative measures and then select those that produce the best results for the main study. If a student plans to continue beyond the Master's degree, his Master's research may lead to his Doctoral program (Walter, 1963).

Data Collection: Primary Sources

Questionnaire and Interview Schedule: Questionnaire is used to collect data directly from large groups of people with diverse characteristics. The questionnaire is either given personally to the informants or sent through mail. Generally, a questionnaire consists of several types of questions and scales. It should be prepared to be suitable to the comprehensive level of the respondents. Characteristics of a Good Questionnaire are:

1. It deals with a specific topic that the respondent will recognize as important enough to spend his time on.
2. It seeks only that information that cannot be obtained from others sources.
3. It should be attractive and well arranged.
4. It should be as short as possible, only long enough to get the essential data.
5. Complete and clear direction should be given. Each question should deal with a single idea. All questions should be worded as simple and as clear as possible.
6. The questions should be objective, with no leading suggestions as to the responses desired.
7. It should be proceeding form general to specific responses.
8. It should be easy to tabulate and interpret.

(Best, 1977).

Interview is an important technique in data collection. It is considered the best way/device of collecting data. It suits well to study the personality characteristics of individuals. Interviews are helpful to study the opinion, attitudes and values of people. "Interview is the purposeful conversation between the interviewer and respondents, initiated for specific purposes and focused on certain planned content areas". (Young & Schmind 1975). Standardized interviews use schedules which are prepared after careful planning and discussion to get answers for the research problem. Case study method is the intensive study of unexplored areas of human behavior. It is concerned with the personal experiences of the individual and to understand the behavior patterns of a particular individual by getting the detailed account in depth. The focus may be on individuals, on situations, on groups or on communities.

Secondary Source/Documentary Sources

It is not always necessary to collect data from the field directly. The needed data may be got from the information, which were collected already for different purpose. Personal letters, diaries, log and other government documents, periodicals like census, health statistics, statistical records, etc. are called Secondary Sources. This type of data is not considered inferior. Since these secondary data are readymade and time saving, they are commonly used in research. The contents of newspapers, magazines, books, journals, radio and television programs also provide a rich source of data. Sometimes they are not found authentic and their accuracy and representation may be poor.

Data Processing/ Analyzing the Results

Coding the responses, tabulating the data and performing statistical computation are done in analysis. More care is taken for economy and to provide safeguard against errors.

Diagrammatic and Graphic Representation

Graphs and charts play a significant role in presenting the research report more clearly and precisely. They explain new and significant relationship between variables and help to discover new ideas and in developing hypothesis.

Interpretation and Conclusion

(a) Reporting

Researcher has to report his findings as accurately and completely as possible. The implications of the findings should be brought out keeping in mind the limitations of the study. He has to provide all the evidences relevant to the research problem. While writing the report, he has to reduce the data and the findings in a condensed form.

(b) Summary

The summary of the report is the restating of the outline of the problem, the procedures, the major findings and conclusions briefly.

(c) Appendices

An appendix usually contains technical materials like general tables, questionnaires or the interview schedule and other matters like measurement procedures.

(d) Bibliographical References

All relevant published and unpublished documents, which are used in the report are included here. Citations should follow a uniform style with enough details for a reader to locate easily the original sources (Walter, 1963).

Steps in Research Writing

- The researcher will get an outline of his report while doing the tabulation.
- He has to decide the nature of information to be conveyed.
- After discussion with other scholars and the supervisor/guide, the outline can be modified.
- Take 2 or 3 drafts of the research report before it is finalized.
- The report has to be edited and rewritten until it gets a good shape.
- The report has to be simple and clear.
- Simple sentences are the best to convey the idea effectively.
- The rules of grammar have to be followed.
- Correct spelling and appropriate punctuating marks should be used.

- Use the present tense rather than the past tense.
- Make direct and positive sentences.
- Number all chapters, sections, sub-sections, tables, and charts
- Use footnotes/ endnotes sparingly, number them serially and give them at the bottom of respective pages or at the end of each chapter. The rules of the footnotes/ endnotes should be followed.
- It is essential to have a good dictionary, good source book and a publication manual for writing the report.
- Be open to Constructive Criticism.
- Incorporate it in the final report.
- The researcher can give some suggestions for further research or point out some problems, which were not covered.

(Isaac & Michel, 1982).

Structure of the Report/ Thesis

The structure of the Report is important since it explains clearly the various aspects of the study. It helps other researchers to evaluate the study in the proper perspective and to interpret it seriously. The content of the report is almost the same as the structure of the research itself. The content of the report consists of the problem, the methodology and the result. The outline is given below.

1. Title Page.
2. Foreword/Acknowledgement.
3. Table of Contents.
4. List of Tables.
5. Introduction or Statement of the Problem.
   (a) Theory, Hypotheses, Definitions, concepts.
   (b) Previous works done, Related Literature.
6. Body of the thesis
   (a) Sample and Sampling Method.
   (b) Respondents.

(c) Data Collection Procedure.

(d) Data Collection Instrument.

(e) Operational Definition of Variables.

(f) Pilot Study.

(g) Methods of Analysis and Statistics.

(h) Field Experience.

(i) Additional Sources of Data.

7. Data Processing and Analysis.
8. Major Findings and Conclusions.
9. Summary.
10. Appendix.
11. Bibliography, Schedule and other Related Materials.

3

HYPOTHESIS AND VARIABLES

Meaning and Significance of a Hypothesis

What is a Hypothesis?

A Hypothesis is usually considered as the principal instrument in research. A hypothesis is a formal question the researcher needs to resolve. It can be defined as a proposition or a set of propositions set forth as an explanation for the occurrence of some specified group of phenomena accepted as highly probable in the light of established facts. In other words, a hypothesis is a provisional formulation or possible solution or tentative explanation or suggested answers to the problem facing the researcher. A hypothesis is tentative, likely to be modified during the investigation if the facts discovered in the course of the enquiry demand it. It is an explanation that needs to be established before it can be accepted.

Functions of Hypothesis

The functions of hypothesis are threefold, namely: (i) to test theories; (ii) to suggest theories and (iii) to describe social phenomena.

1. **To Test Theories:**

   The function of the hypothesis is to state a specific relationship between phenomena in such a way that this relationship can be empirically tested. That is, the hypothesis must be empirically demonstrated as either, probably or not. The theories lend themselves for empirical test only if the facts, proposition and assumption implied in them are split up into specific hypotheses.

2. **To Suggest Theories:**

   Another function of hypothesis is to suggest theories. That

is to say every worthwhile theory permits the formulation of additional hypothesis.These when tested were either proved or disproved and in turn constitute further tests of the original theory.

3. **To Describe Social Phenomena**:

   When hypotheses are tested they explain the phenomena associated with them. The phenomena may be totally new or partly known earlier or not known earlier. Hypothesis helps the researcher to prove, disprove or improve his assumption of proposition.

Forms and Sources of Hypothesis

1. A hypothesis may originate in different ways. A cultural environment may give rise to it. In India, for example, religion and custom dominate the way of life. This has had its reaction on economic values and individual initiatives in various walks of life. Such a situation could give rise to any number of hypotheses, such as sociological, cultural, political and economic, etc.
2. A second source of hypothesis is folk wisdom or current popular beliefs and practices suggesting both the problems and the hypothesis.
3. Analogies are often a spring of valuable hypotheses. Students of sociology in the course of their studies would have come across analogies where in society is compared to a biological organism, the natural law to the social law, thermodynamics to social dynamics, etc.
4. Hypotheses may arise from the findings of other studies.
5. Hypotheses can be formulated from cases which are exceptions to accepted theories.
6. Personal experience and individual reaction can be the basis for hypothesis, a hypothesis may come up from a body of theories which may lead to the prediction that if certain conditions are present, certain results will follow (Kothari, 2009).

Criteria of Workable Hypothesis

All hypotheses are not equally helpful or workable to the enquiry and some are perhaps not at all. The researcher has to separate the more useful ones from the less useful. A good workable hypothesis is one which satisfies many of the following criteria:

1. **Conceptual Clarity**:

   Hypothesis should be clear and precise. If not, the inferences drawn on its basis cannot be taken as reliable. It is advisable that the concepts embodied in hypotheses be clearly defined in a manner commonly accepted and communicable. The conceptual clarity is required both formally as well as operationally. Formal definition or explication of the concepts will clarify what a particular concept stands for, which the operational definition will leave no ambiguity about what would constitute empirical evidence or indicator of the concept in the field.

2. **Empirically Testable:**

   A hypothesis should be empirically testable. It should be so stated that it is possible to deduce logically certain inferences from it, which in turn can be tested by observation in the field.

3. **Closest to Things Observable**:

   Hypothesis should be closest to things observable. Failing this, it would not be possible to test their accord with empirical facts.

4. **Specific in Nature:**

   The hypothesis must be specific in nature (and precise), i.e. it must help to detail all operations and predictions connected with it in the process of investigation. It should not involve the investigator in unnecessary roaming about and discussion.

5. **Related to a Body of Theory**:

   The hypothesis should be related to a body of theory or some theoretical orientation. If the hypothesis is related to some theory, research will help to qualify, support, correct or refute the theory.

6. **Relevant and available techniques:**

   An investigation to be practical should relate the hypothesis to the investigational techniques feasible in the particular science. This requires in the researcher a sound knowledge of techniques to test the hypothesis and to formulate practical questions.

7. **Simple:**

   The hypothesis should be simple and to the point. Insight of the phenomena is essential for simplicity, i.e. the more insight the researcher has into the problem, the simpler will be the hypothesis about it. The better hypothesis is the simple one requiring fewer conditions or assumptions.

8. **Brevity:**

   The hypothesis should be brief so that its observation may be possible. It would help better understanding of the underlying concept and meaning.

9. **State the Expected Relationship between Variables:**

   A satisfactory hypothesis should state explicitly expected relationship between the variables.

10. **Limited in Scope:**

    Hypotheses of global significance are not usable as they are not specific and simple for testing and drawing conclusions. It is desirable to formulate hypotheses that are simple to test and yet are highly significant.

11. **Consistent with most known facts:**

    Hypotheses should not be inconsistent with substantial body of established facts.They should be grounded in the well established theory.

Difficulties in Formulation of Hypothesis

The task of formulation of hypothesis has certain difficulties, such as:

1. **Lack of Clear Theoretical Background:**

   If hypotheses do not have a clear-cut and definite theoretical background, it is not easy to arrive at certain conclusions.

2. Lack of Logical Background:

Sometimes a hypothesis not only lacks a definite and clear-cut background, and lacks the logical use of the theoretical background. It means that there is no logical background.

3. Lack of Knowledge of Scientific Methods:

It is not always possible to have complete information of an acquaintance with the scientific methods for formulation of hypotheses. This lack of scientific knowledge presents difficulty in formulation of hypotheses.

Steps to Remove Difficulties with the Formulation of Hypothesis

1. Complete and perfect knowledge of the principles of research has to be acquired.
2. From the very beginning, the hypothesis should be brief and timely, and
3. It should grow as the research proceeds further. In other words, it means hypothesis should become elaborate as one proceeds in the field of research.

Utility of Hypothesis

The utility or importance of hypothesis for research may be summed as follows:

1. Hypothesis provides guidance to proceed on certain definite lines:

Hypothesis helps the investigator in knowing the direction in which he should proceed. In the absence of hypothesis, the researcher is like a sailor on a vessel in the sea without a compass or rudder.

2. Hypothesis helps in selecting pertinent factors:

Once the investigator is able to get the direction with the help of the hypothesis, he is able to eliminate the irrelevant facts and concentrate only on relevant and pertinent facts."The use of hypothesis prevents a blind search and indiscriminate gathering of masses of data which may later prove irrelevant to the problem under study."

3. Hypothesis helps in drawing specific conclusions:

If hypothesis is rightly drawn and scientifically formulated, it helps the researcher not only to proceed with his study on right lines but also to draw conclusions (Saravanavel, 2005).

Testing the Hypothesis

Testing the hypothesis means subjecting it to some sort of empirical scrutiny to determine if it is supported or refuted by what the researcher observes. There are two pre-requisites to test a hypothesis:

1. A real social situation is needed that will suffice as a reasonable testing ground for the hypothesis, and
2. The investigator should make sure that the hypothesis is testable.

There are two fairly important means of testing a hypothesis, namely:

1. The study of the hypothesis for logical consistency, and
2. The study of hypothesis for agreement with fact.

The study of hypotheses consists of checking the logical character of the reasoning by which the consequences of hypotheses are deduced for verification. In the second place the study of hypothesis for logical consistency involves checking it for agreement with the already known laws of nature. It must not conflict with the highest and simplest laws of good thinking and it must not disagree with those principles of science which are considered valid beyond reasonable doubt. The suggested inferences are tested in thought, for logical coherence, before they are tested in action. In the study of hypothesis for agreement with fact, one argues that if the hypothesis is true, certain facts, conditions or relationship will be found, then one looks to see if these conditions are present. After testing the hypothesis by applying it to already known facts, it may have to be tested by a new appeal to experience. In this new appeal, the data are collected, recorded and interpreted according to the conventions of science. If the data already available are adequate, no new appeal to experience will be necessary.

Hypothesis Testing and Statistical Significance

1. The Research Hypothesis and the Null Hypothesis

(a) The research hypothesis states the expectations of the researcher in positive terms. It identifies the variables or conditions which, in casual relationship, will be advanced to account for the results and is often derived from a theory.

(b) The null hypothesis – the hypothesis of "no relationship or difference" – is the one actually tested statistically. It is an arbitrary convention hypothesizing that any relation or difference in the findings is due to chance or sampling error and puts this supposition to a probability test. Theoretically, it is an hypothesis set up for possible rejection and though the degree of relationship or margin of difference need not be zero, it frequently is.

2. Stating the Null Hypothesis

There are four alternatives, using the example of the difference between two samples which means:

(a) There is no difference between the means of the two populations from which the two samples were drawn at random.

(b) The two means in the two populations from which the samples were respectively drawn at random are equal.

(c) The mean of the sampling distribution of differences between an infinite number of pairs of means of randomly drawn samples equals zero.

(d) Any difference between two samples means drawn randomly from their respective populations is due to sampling error – that is, such differences can readily be attributed to chance.

3. Accepting or Rejecting the Null Hypothesis – What it Means

Testing the null hypothesis results in one of two outcomes:

(a) Accepting (failing to reject) the null hypothesis as true, in which case it is concluded that any differences in the results are:

(1) Not statistically significant, therefore are probably accepted.

(2) Due to sampling error or chance.

(b) Rejecting the null hypothesis as false, in which case it is concluded that the differences in the results are:

(1) Statistically significant, therefore are probably rejected.

(2) Due to some determining factor or condition, other than chance.

Accepting the null hypothesis also means that the corresponding research hypothesis is not supported or disconfirmed. Rejecting the null hypothesis also means the corresponding research hypothesis has survived a test of disconfirmation and, in that sense, is supported. More precisely, the differences in the data reasonably cannot be attributed to chance and the causal factors stated in the research hypothesis may possibly explain the difference, but not necessarily so long as there are plausible rival hypothesis also to account for the data. Obviously, the more tests of disconfirmation a given research hypothesis can survive, the stronger is the evidence in its support.

4. Accepting or Rejecting the Null Hypothesis – Two types of Errors

(a) Type I (Alpha) Error – to reject the null hypothesis of no differences when it is true. In other words, to conclude falsely that a difference exists in the data when in fact it does not. Since such an error is particularly embarrassing to the researcher (saying something exists when it does not), he tends to avoid risking this error and chooses a conservative level of significance which minimizes it.

(b) Type II (Beta) Error – to accept the null hypothesis of no difference when it is false. In other words, to conclude falsely that a difference does not exist in the data when in fact it does.

(c) The decision between risks – Whether to run the risk of a Type I or Type II error, since the probability of one increases as the other decreases, is a question of utility. Which is preferable in a given situation: (1) a Type I fine screen designed to eliminate chance differences at the expense of throwing away some genuine differences in the process? Or (2) a Type II coarse screen that lets through some of the unwanted chance differences to insure that most of the genuine differences are kept? When the consequences of mistaking a chance difference for a genuine difference are too costly and the risk of such an error must be minimized, a conservative level of significance is set, avoiding the Type I error. When, on the other hand, there is a search for all promising leads and no genuine prospect can be overlooked, a liberal level of significance is selected, avoiding the Type II error. Note: To avoid the probability of either error, increase the sample size, N.

5. Rejecting the Null Hypothesis and Theory Building

The task of theory-building and data analysis is to reject inadequate hypothesis. Experimental findings never confirm or prove a theory. Rather, the successful theory is tested and escapes being disconfirmed and the more tests of this nature it survives, the stronger it stands. Strictly speaking, the null hypothesis can never be accepted – it can only be rejected or fail to be rejected.

6. One-tailed and Two-tailed Tests of the Null Hypothesis

When a particular research hypothesis simply predicts that a difference will exist in the data and allows this difference to be in either direction (larger or smaller), it is a two tailed test of its null hypothesis counterpart, since the difference can fall in the tail of this sampling distribution. If, on the other hand, the research hypothesis predicts the direction of the difference (either larger or smaller), it is a one-tailed test of the corresponding null hypothesis.

7. The Power of a Statistical Test

The power of a statistical test is defined as the probability of rejecting the null hypothesis of no differences when it is actually false. In other words, differences really do exist, and the null hypothesis ought to be rejected.

Power = 1 – probability of Type II error

The power of a statistical test is a function of:

(a) The underlying assumptions of the test: parametric tests make stronger assumptions than nonparametric tests.

(b) Whether the test is one-tailed (often more powerful in a certain region of admissible alternative hypotheses of interest) or two-tailed (less powerful in that same region).

(c) Sample size N: as N increases, power usually increases. Power efficiency refers to the increase in sample size necessary to make test X as powerful as a second test Y.

8. Level of Significance and Replication

While the conventional level for rejecting the null hypothesis is p=.05 or .01 (5 percent and 1 percent, respectively), significance levels of 10 to 20 percent are tolerable in preliminary investigations, with replication. Note: If two successive findings are each significant at the 10 percent level, this is roughly equivalent to a single finding at the 1 percent level since the two kinds of outcomes are about equally probable. Moreover, replication provides empirically stronger evidence than a single occurrence and justifies the more liberal test of the null hypothesis, avoiding the Type II error.

9. Statistical Significance Versus Practical Significance

In the researcher's zeal to obtain statistically significant findings, he often overlooks the more relevant question: Is it educationally significant? Is the difference large enough to be practical? Are the gains important enough to be worth the cost and effort to obtain them? This question gets at the trade off factor in educational decision making and involves the problem of accountability in cost effectiveness economics. Even when these practical matters are settled or in the background, there are valuable considerations of social and psychological nature that frequently override a choice based solely on statistical significance. (Saravanavel 2005)

Variables

One need to know about variables because quantitative researchers usually describe the world by using variables and they attempt to explain and predict aspects of the world by demonstrating the relationships among variables. we can see a summary of the types of variables in Table 3.1.

Table – 3.1

Common Types of Variables Classified by level of Measurement and Role of Variable

Variable Type	*Key Characteristic*	*Example*
Level of measurement Categorical variable	A variable that is made up of different types or categories of a pheno-menon.	The variable gender is made up of the categories of male and female.
Quantitative variable	A variable that varies in degree or amount of a phenomenon	The variable annual income varies from zero income to a very high income level
Role Taken by the Variable		
Independent variable	A variable that is presumed to cause changes to occur in another variable, a causal variable.	Amount of studying affects test grades.
Dependent variable	A variable that chang-es because of another variable, the effect or outcome variable.	Amount of studying affects grades.
Meditating variable (It is also called an intervening variable)	A variable that comes in between other variables, helps to delineate the process through which variables affect one another.	Amount of studying leads to input and organization of kno-wledge in longterm memory (mediating variable), which affects test grades.

Moderator variable	A variable that delineates how a relationship of interest changes under different conditions or circumstances.	Perhaps the relationship between studying and test grades changes according to the different levels of use of a drug such as Ritalin (moderator).

Source: Monash University, Ph.D. Guidelines, 2009.

A **variable** is a condition or characteristic that can take on different values or categories. A much-studied educational variable is intelligence, which varies from low to high for different people. Age is another variable that varies from low to high. Another variable is gender, which is either male or female. To better understand the concept of a variable, it is helpful to compare it with a constant, its opposite. A constant is a single value or category of a variable. Here's the idea: The variable gender is a marker for two constants: male and female. The category (i.e., constant) male is a marker for only one thing; it is one of the two constants forming the variable called gender. Gender varies, but male does not vary. Therefore, gender is a variable and male is a constant. In the case of the variable age, all of the ages make up the values (i.e., constant) of the variable and each value (e.g., twelve years old or thirteen years old) is a constant. If a researcher is still having a hard time with the distinction between a variable and a constant, think of it like this: A variable is like a set of things and a constant is one of those things.

Yet another categorization scheme for variables is to speak of independent and dependent variables. An independent variable is a variable that is presumed to cause a change in another variable. Some times the independent variable is manipulated by the researcher (i.e., the researcher determines the value of the independent variable); at other times, the independent variable is studied by the researcher but is not directly manipulated (i.e., the researcher studies what happens when an independent variable changes naturally).

The variables that just used age and gender, are actually different types of variables. Age is an example of a quantitative variable and gender is an example of a categorical variable. A quantitative variable is a variable that varies in degree or amount. It usually involves numbers. A categorical variable is a variable that varies in type or kind. It usually involves different groups. As described in the previous paragraph, age takes on numbers (e.g., numbers of years old) and gender takes on two types or kinds (male and female). Now consider the variable annual income. How does it vary? It varies in amount, ranging from no income at all to some very large amount of income. Therefore, income is a quantitative variable. If a researcher thinks about how much money one made last year, he can determine his value on the variable annual income. Now think about the variable religion. How does this variable vary? It varies in kind or type. It can take on any of the categories standing for the different world religions (e.g., Hinduism, Christianity, Judaism, and Islam). If the researcher needs a little more practice identifying quantitative and categorical variables, take a look at the examples in Table. 3.2.

Table 3.2

Examples of Quantitative and Categorical Variables

Quantitative Variables	*Categorical Variables*
Height	Gender
Weight	Religion
Temperature	Ethnicity
Annual income	Method of therapy
Most aptitude tests	College major
Most achievement tests	Political party identification
School size	Type of school
Class size	Marital status of parents
Self-esteem level	Student retention (retained or not)
Grade point average	Type of teacher expectation
Teacher -pupil ratio	Native language
Time spent on homework	Teaching method

Age	Personality type
Anxiety level	Learning style
Job satisfaction score	Type of feedback
Number of behavioral outbursts	Computer use (or not)
Reading performance	Type of reading instruction
Spelling accuracy	Inclusion (or not)
Number of performance errors	Problem solving strategy used
Rate of cognitive processing	Memory strategy used
Dropout rate	Social class

Source: Monash University, Ph.D. Guidelines, 2009.

The independent variable is an antecedent variable because it must come before another variable if it is to produce a change in it. A dependent variable is the variable that is presumed to be influenced by one or more independent variables. The dependent variable is the variable that is "dependent on" the independent (i.e., antecedent) variable(s). A cause-and-effect relationship between an independent and a dependent variable is present when changes in the independent variable an outcome variable or a response variable because it is used to measure the effect of one or more independent variables.

Here is a simple example of a cause-and-effect relationship. Smoking Causes Lung Cancer, Heart Disease, Emphysema and may complicate pregnancy. Can you identify the independent and dependent variables in this relationship? It is smoking that is presumed to cause lung cancer and several other diseases. (One should be aware that extensive research beyond simply observing that smoking and lung cancer were associated was conducted to establish that the link between smoking and cancer was causal.) In this example, smoking is the independent variable (the values corresponding to the number of cigarettes smoked a day) and presence of lung cancer is the dependent variable (the values being lung cancer present and lung cancer not present). (Monash University, Ph.D. Research Guidelines, 1999).

4

RESEARCH DESIGN AND SAMPLE DESIGN

Research Design

Need for Research Design

Research design is needed because it facilitates the smooth sailing of the various research operations, thereby making research as efficient as possible yielding maximal information with minimal expenditure of effort, time and money. Just as for better economical and attractive construction of a house, we need a blueprint (or what is commonly called the map of the house) well thought out and prepared by an expert architect, we need a research design or a plan in advance of data collection and analysis for our research project. Research design stands for advance planning of the methods to be adopted for collecting the relevant data and the techniques to be used in their analysis, keeping in view the objective of the research and the availability of staff, time and money. Preparation of the research design should be done with great care as any error in it may upset the entire project. Research design, in fact, has a great bearing on the reliability of the results arrived at and as such constitutes the firm foundation of the entire edifice of the research work. Research design is a catalogue of the various phases and facts relating to the formulation of a research effort. It is the arrangement of conditions for collection and analysis of data in a manner that aims to combine relevance to the research purpose with economy in procedure.

Meaning of Research Design

An architect prepares a blue-print before he approves a construction. An army prepares a strategy before launching an attack. An artist makes a plan before he executes his ideas. So also the researcher makes a plan of his study before he undertakes his research work. This will enable the researcher to save time and resources. Such a plan of study or blueprint for study is called a Research Design or Research Strategy. A researcher attempting to solve his problem should necessarily prepare a plan which will help him to attain his ultimate motto. This plan is nothing but a research design.It is a plan for the collection and analysis of data. It is a tentative plan, which undergoes many modifications as the study progresses. It presents a series of guide posts to enable the researcher to progress in the right direction. It gives an outline of the structure and process of the research program. Without such a plan of study no scientific study is possible. It is a crucial step in the dissertation or thesis because, if a wrong decision is made, the whole study may be criticized on the grounds of inappropriate design or even worse as being unscientific or illogical. A research design should be based more or less on some methodology. The research design should be made once the topic and problem of research have been selected and formulated, objectives have been properly outlined, concepts have been properly defined and the hypothesis or hypotheses have been properly framed. (Saravanavel, 2009).

A Research Design should be able to Provide Answers to the following Queries:

1. What is the study about and, what type of data is required?
2. What is the purpose of the study? What is its scope?
3. What are the sources of the needed data?
4. What should be the place or area of the study?
5. What time, approximately is required for the study?
6. What should be the amount of material or number of cases for the study?
7. What types of sampling should be used?
8. What method of data collection would be appropriate?
9. How will the data be analyzed?
10. What should be the approximate expenditure?
11. What should be the methodology of the study?
12. What should be the specific nature of the study?

The process of study is best promoted by a research design or plan, which can be of definite help in achieving optimum objectivity, efficiency and reliability. However, any research design is only tentative in the sense that as the study progresses, new facts, new ideas and new conditions may make their appearance, which may necessitate a change in the original paradigm. Thus, a research design cannot be an inflexible paradigm.

A methodologically designed research may lead to the following advantages:

1. It may result in the desired type of study with useful conclusions;
2. It may lead to more accurate result, or help to reduce inaccuracy;
3. It may give optimum efficiency and reliability;
4. It may minimize the wastage of time, and beating around the bush;
5. It may minimize the uncertainty, confusion and practical hazards associated with any research problem;
6. It may be helpful for the collection of research material and testing of hypothesis, and
7. A research design is a guide post for giving research a right direction.

Keeping in View the Necessary Design Decision, one can Split the Overall Research Design into the following Parts.

1. The Sample Design which deals with the method of selecting items to be observed for the given study;
2. The Observational Design which relates to the conditions under which the observations are to be made;
3. The Statistical Design which concerns with the question of how many items are to be observed and how the information and data gathered are to be analyzed; and
4. The Operational Design, which deals with the techniques by which the procedures specified in the sampling, statistical and observational designs, can be carried out. (Kothari, 2009).

From what has been stated above, we can state the Important Features of Research Design as follows:

1. It is a plan that specifies the sources and types of information relevant to the research problem;
2. It is a strategy specifying which approach will be used for gathering and analyzing the data; and
3. It also includes the time and cost budget since most studies are done under these two constraints.

In brief, Research Design Must, at Least, Contain

1. A clear statement of the research problem;
2. Procedures and techniques to be used for gathering information;
3. The population to be studied; and
4. Methods to be used in processing and analyzing data.

Evaluation of the Research Design

The fundamental questions in evaluating a research design pertain to the precision, reliability and relevance of the data and their analysis. Before actually carrying out research, it is better if the investigator re-evaluates his research design.This can be achieved if the investigator verifies the following aspects for the explicitness.

1. How precise are the observations?
2. Can other investigators repeat the observations?
3. How explicit are the hypotheses?
4. Have the problems and hypotheses been stated in operational terms scientifically?
5. Has the plan or research been presented in detail so that its logic is apparent?
6. Do the data actually satisfy the demands of the problem i.e., do they actually demonstrate the conclusion?
7. Does the research design ensure a comparison that is not subject to the alternative interpretations?

Research design can be of definite help in achieving optimum objectivity, efficiency and reliability. A methodologically designed research may lead to the advantages of useful conclusions, more accuracy, optimum efficiency and reliability, avoid wastage of time, minimize the uncertainty, confusion and practical hazards, help to collect research material and test hypothesis. A research design is a guide post for giving research a right direction.

The Research design must be carefully planned so that subjective bias can be eliminated.

1. Decide the objectives.
2. Data collection – (1) Use of documents (2) Observation (3) Interviews and questionnaires – Selection depends upon the objective.

Analysis and Interpretation

The process of analyzing the data includes coding the responses, i.e., placing the data according to their categories.

In the descriptive/diagnostic studies, the structure and observational design, the sampling design, statistical design, and operational design also remain rigid. In exploratory study these are flexible.

Experimental Design

It is concerned with making experiments to find out the cause effect relationship of the phenomenon under study. The main purpose is to test the causal hypothesis. It is considered to be the highest stage of social research.

1. The experimental method reduces personal bias and also it helps to draw inferences.
2. These are hypothesis testing studies.

The researcher tests the hypotheses of causal relationship between variables.

Basic Principles of Experimental Design

The principle of Replication – Experiment should be repeated.

Example: Two varieties of rice are taken to test their quality for fixing the price.

The Principle of Randomization

It provides protection, when we conduct an experiment, against the effects of extraneous factors by randomization. We should plan the experiment in such a way that the variables caused by extraneous factors can all be combined under the general heading of 'Chance'.

Example: We may assign the variety of rice to be grown in different parts of the field on the basis of some random sampling technique. Fertility difference will give wrong results.

The Principle of Local Control

Under it the extraneous factor, the known source of variability is made to vary deliberately over as wide a range as necessary. This needs to be done in such a way that the variability it causes can be measured and hence eliminated from the experimental error.

EXPERIMENTAL DESIGN

After only | Before after | Ex–post facto | Panel study

After Only Experimental Design

In this design, the experimental group and the control group are similar. The uncontrolled external factors may affect both the groups equally.

The experimental group is exposed to the assumed causal variable (x), but the control group is not exposed.

After the experimentation is over, both groups are compared and it may be noticed that some effect (Y) has produced in the experimental group but not in the control group.

X–cause; y–Effect. Only after the experimental design is tested the two groups are assumed to be exactly similar.

Before –After Experimental Design

In this design, the dependent variable, i.e., effect is measured both before and after the exposure of group to experiment.

When there are two groups–one experimental group and the other control group–both of them are measured at the beginning and also at the end of the experimental period. However, experimental variable is introduced only in the experimental group. Since both the groups are subject to before 'measurement' and the uncontrolled factors, the difference between the two group is regarded as the effect of experimental variable alone.

Condition	*Experiment Group*	*Control Group*
Before Measurement	Yes (Y_1)	Yes (y_1)
Exposure to experiment	Yes	No
Exposure to uncontrolled factors	Yes	Yes
After measurement	Yes (Y_2)	Yes (y_2)
Change	($Y_2 - Y_1$)	($Y_2 - Y_1$)

Ex-Post Facto Design

Sometimes it is not possible to divide population into two clear and similar groups.This may be the case where the entire society consisting of different varieties of people are involved.

For example, the researcher is interested in studying the causes of a revolution which has already occurred. This will be done through ex-post facto.

The researcher should select two countries – one in which revolution has taken place and the other where is has not. But similar countries are difficult to find.

Panel Study

Panel study is a method of studying a particular subject overtime by using different kinds of data. It involves repeated observations in the same subject at different periods of time.

It is a type of **Time – Series study.**

Panel study is continuous, thorough, deep and reliable.

Conclusion

A research design should contain

1. Topic of research
2. Objectives and Hypothesis

3. Concepts and their Operational definitions
4. Variables
5. Methods of Data collection
6. Methods of Data processing

Table 4.1
Research Design

Research Design Overall Design	*Exploratory Flexible Design*	*Descriptive/ Diagnostic Rigid Design*
1. Sample Design.	Purposive or judgment sampling.	Probability sampling design / random sampling.
2. Statistical Design.	Non pre-planned design for analysis.	Pre-planned design for analysis.
3. Observation Design.	Un-structural instruments for collection of data.	Structural instruments.
4. Operational Design.	Non fixed decisions about the operational procedures.	Advanced decisions about operational procedures.

Sample

When field studies are undertaken in practical life, considerations of time and cost almost invariably lead to a selection of respondents i.e., selection of only a few items.The respondents selected should be as representative of the total population as possible in order to produce a miniature cross-section.The selected respondents constitute what is technically called a 'sample' and the selection process is called 'sampling technique.' The survey so conducted is known as 'sample survey'. Algebraically, let the population size be N and if a part of size n (which is<N) of this population is selected according to some rule for studying some characteristics of the population, the group consisting of these n units is known as 'sample'. Researcher must prepare a sample design for his study i.e., he/she must plan how a sample should be selected and of what size such a sample would be.

Sample Design

In social sciences we are usually interested in discovering something about a real world phenomenon that we assume already exists. These real world phenomena can be anything in economic, social, political or behavior. What ever the phenomenon we desire to explain, we seek to explain it by collecting data from the real world, and then using the data to draw conclusions about what is being studied. If we collect and analyze data from every possible case or group member i.e., a complete enumeration of all units in a population (the full set of cases for which we want to generalize about a phenomenon) is known as census inquiry and this involves great deal of time and money. In addition, the errors in survey, measurement and results will be larger. Sampling techniques provide a range of methods that enable us to reduce the amount of data we need to collect by considering only data from a sub group rather than all possible cases or elements. Thus sampling method is normally used to save time and money and to minimize the error in any statistical investigation. Sampling is a tool, which enables to draw conclusions about the characteristics of the population after studying only those objects, or items that are included in the sample. A sample is a miniature picture or smaller representation of the entire group or population.

A sample design is a definite plan for obtaining a sample from a given population. It refers to the technique or the procedure the researcher would adopt in selecting items for the sample. Sample design may as well lay down the number of items to be included in the sample i.e., the size of the sample. Sample design is determined before data are collected. There are many sample designs from which a researcher can choose. Some designs are relatively more precise and easier to apply than others. Researcher must select/prepare a sample design which should be reliable and appropriate for his/her research study.

A sample design refers to a definite plan for obtaining a sample from a population. A good sample design posses the following characteristics:

1. The sample design must result in a truly typical or representative sample.
2. The sampling error should be as small as possible.
3. It should be viable in the context of available resources.
4. The systematic bias can be controlled in a better way.
5. The results obtained from the sample can be applied to the universe with a reasonable confidence level.

Steps in Sample Design

While developing a sample design, the researcher must pay attention to the following points:

1. Type of Universe: The first step in developing any sample design is to clearly define the set of objects, technically called the Universe, to be studied. The universe can be finite or the number of items is infinite. i.e., we cannot have any idea about the total number of items. The population of a city, the number of workers in a factory and the like are examples of finite universes, whereas the number of stars in the sky, listeners of a specific radio program, throwing of a dice etc. are examples of infinite universes.

2. Sampling Unit: A decision has to be taken concerning a sampling unit before selecting sample. Sampling unit may be a geographical one such as state, district, village, etc., or a construction unit such as house, flat, etc., or it may be a social unit such as family, club, school, etc., or it may be an individual. The researcher will have to decide one or more of such units that has to be selected for his study.

3. Source List: It is also known as 'sampling frame' from which sample is to be drawn. It contains the names of all items of a universe (in case of finite universe only). If source list is not available, researcher has to prepare it. Such a list should be comprehensive, correct, reliable and appropriate. It is extremely important for the source list to be as representative of the population as possible.

4. Size of Sample: It refers to the number of items to be selected from the universe to constitute a sample. This is a major problem before a researcher. The size of sample should neither be excessively large, nor too small. It should be optimum. An optimum sample is one which fulfills the requirements of efficiency, representativeness, reliability and flexibility. While deciding the size of sample, researcher must determine the desired precision as also an acceptable confidence level for the estimate. The size of population variance needs to be considered as in case of larger variance usually a bigger sample is needed. The size of population must be kept in view, while deciding the size of the sample. Costs too dictate the size of sample that we can draw. As such, budgetary constraint must invariably be taken into consideration when we decide the sample size.

5. Parameter of Interest: In determining the sample design, one must consider the question of the specific population parameters which are of interest. For instance, we may be interested in estimating the proportion of persons with some characteristic in the population, or we may be interested in knowing some average or the other measure concerning the population. There may also be important subgroups in the population about whom we would like to make estimates. All this has a strong impact upon the sample design we would accept.

6. Budgetary Constraint: Cost considerations from practical point of view, have a major impact upon decisions relating to not only the size of the sample but also to the type of sample. This fact can even lead to the use of a non-probability sample.

7. Sampling Procedure: Finally, the researcher must decide the type of sample he will use i.e., he must decide about the technique to be used in selecting the items for the sample. In fact, this technique or procedure stands for the sample design itself. There are several sample designs (explained in the pages that follow) out of which the researcher must choose one for his study. Obviously, he must select that design which, for a given sample size and for a given cost, has a smaller sampling error. (Kothari, 2009)

Criteria of Selecting a Sampling Procedure

In this context one must remember that two costs are involved in a sampling analysis viz., the cost of collecting the data and the cost of an incorrect inference resulting from the data. Researcher must keep in view the two causes of incorrect inferences viz., systematic bias and sampling error. A systematic bias results from errors in the sampling procedures and it cannot be reduced or eliminated by increasing the sample size. At best the causes responsible for these errors can be detected and corrected. Usually a systematic bias is the result of one or more of the following factors:

1. Inappropriate Sampling Frame: If the sampling frame is inappropriate i.e., a biased representation of the universe, it will result in a systematic bias.

2. Defective Measuring Device: If the measuring device is constantly in error, it will result in systematic bias. In survey work, systematic bias can result if the questionnaire or the interviewer is biased. Similarly, if the physical measuring device is defective there will be systematic bias in the data collected through such a measuring device.

3. Non-respondents: If we are unable to sample all the individuals initially included in the sample, there may arise a systematic bias. The reason is that in such a situation the likelihood of establishing contact or receiving a response from an individual is often correlated with the measure of what is to be estimated.

4. Indeterminacy Principle: Sometimes we find that individuals act differently when kept under observation than what they do when kept in non-observed situation. For instance, if workers are aware that somebody is observing them in course of a work study on the basis of which the average length of time to complete a task will be determined and accordingly the quota will be set for piece work, they generally tend to work slowly in comparison to the speed with which they work if kept unobserved. Thus, the indeterminacy principle may also be a cause of a systematic bias.

5. Natural bias in the Reporting of Data: Natural bias of respondents in the reporting of data is often the cause of a systematic bias in many inquiries. There is usually a downward bias in the income data collected by government taxation department, whereas we find an upward bias in the income data collected by some social organization. People in general understate their incomes if asked about it for tax purposes, but they overstate the same if asked for social status or their affluence. Generally in psychological surveys, people tend to give what they think is the 'correct' answer rather than revealing their true feelings. (Kothari, 1999).

Sampling errors are the random variations in the sample estimates around the true population parameters. Since they occur randomly and are equally likely to be in either direction, their nature happens to be of compensatory type and the expected value of such errors happens to be equal to zero. Sampling error decreases with the increase in the size of the sample, and it happens to be of a smaller magnitude in case of homogeneous population.

Sampling error can be measured for a given sample design and size. The measurement of sampling error is usually called the 'precision of the sampling plan.' If we increase the sample size, the precision can be improved. But increasing the size of the sample has its own limitations viz., a large sized sample increases the cost of collecting data and also enhances the systematic bias. Thus the effective way to increase precision is usually to select a better sample design which has a smaller sampling error for a given sample size at a given sample size at a given cost. In practice, however, people prefer a less precise design because it is easier to adopt the same and also because of the fact that systematic bias can be controlled in a better way in such a design.

In brief, while selecting a sampling procedure, researcher must ensure that the procedure causes a relatively small sampling error and helps to control the systematic bias in a better way.

Characteristics of a Good Sample Design

From what has been stated above, we can list down the characteristics of a good sample design as under:

1. Sample design must result in a truly representative sample.
2. Sample design must be such which results in a small sampling error.
3. Sample design must be viable in the context of funds available for the research study.
4. Sample design must be such so that systematic bias can be controlled in a better way.

5. Sample should be such that the results of the sample study can be applied, in general, for the universe with a reasonable level of confidence. (Kothari, 2009).

The Process of Sampling

The process of sampling can be divided into the following four stages.

1. Identify a suitable Sampling and select the sample.
2. Decide on a suitable sample size.
3. Select the most appropriate sampling and select the sample.
4. Check that the sample is representative of the population.

1. Sampling Frame

A sample frame is a complete list of all the cases or units in the population from which the samples can be selected at each sampling stage. It is very important and influences every aspect of the sampling design viz., the population coverage, the stages of sampling, the stratification used and the process of selection itself.

2. Sample Size

Apart from the choice of the sampling method, the researcher is very much concerned with the sample size. If the sample size is too small, the experiment will lack the precision to provide reliable answers to the questions it is investigating. If the sample size is too large, time and resources will be wasted, often of marginal gain. The basic postulate worth remembering is that there is no relationship between the size of the target population and the size of the sample.

The major considerations in determining the size of the sample are:

(a) Viability of the population.

(b) The desired precision (margin of error).

(c) The degree of confidence; and

(d) The cost of the survey.

Determining the size of the sample involves a trade off between variability, precision, and confidence on the one hand and the cost of the survey on the other. However, the general advice of minimum number of 30 for statistical analysis provides a useful rule of thumb for the smallest number in each category within an overall sample.

3. Sampling Technique

The available sampling techniques for the selection of a sample from the population can be divided into two types.

Viz. (a) Probability or Random Sampling and

(b) Non-probability or non-random sampling.

With probability samples, the chance or probability of each case being selected from the population is known and is equal for all cases. Hence, it is possible to answer research questions and to achieve objectives that require estimating statistically the characteristics of the population from the sample. For non-probability sample, the probability of each case being selected from the total population is not known and it is impossible to answer research questions or to make statistical inferences about the characteristics of the population.

Probability Sampling Methods

1. ***Simple Random Sampling:*** It involves selecting the sample at random from the sampling frame using lottery method or random number tables or a computer.
2. ***Stratified Random Sampling:*** In this method the population is divided into a number of relevant and significant data based on one or a number of attributes. A random sample is then drawn from each of the data.
3. ***Systematic Random Sampling:*** It involves selecting the sample at regular intervals from the sampling frame.
4. ***Cluster Sampling:*** In this method we need to divide the population into discrete groups, termed as clusters, prior to sampling. For cluster sampling method, the sampling frame is the complete list of clusters rather than a complete list of individual cases within the population.Then we select a few clusters randomly, and collect the data from every case within the selected clusters.
5. ***Multi-stage Random Sampling:*** It is some times called as

multi-stage cluster sampling; and it is a development of cluster sampling.

Non-Probability Sampling Methods

1. ***Purposive or Judgment Samplings:*** In this method we sample with a purpose in mind. It enables us to use our judgment to select cases that will best enable us to answer our research questions and to meet our objectives.
2. ***Convenience Sampling:*** Convenience is haphazard sampling which involves selecting haphazardly those cases that are easiest for obtain for our sample.
3. ***Quota Sampling:*** It is normally used for interview surveys in which we select cases non-randomly according to some fixed quota. The two types of quota sampling are proportional and non-proportional.
4. ***Expert Sampling:*** It involves the assembling of a sample of elements with known or demonstrable experience and expertise in some area.
5. ***Snowball Sampling:*** It is commonly used when it is difficult to identify members of the desired population.

4. Checking the Representative Sample

Often it is possible to compare data we collect from our sample with data from another source for the population. For example, we can compare data on socio-economic characteristics of respondents with those characteristics for the population in the state or country, as recorded in the latest official documents.

Sampling is a critical component in virtually all social research. In research the key point is not about which sampling method is used but the external validity, i.e., how valid the inferences form the sample. Hence, the main job as a social science researcher is to create sampling strategy that is appropriate to the context and will assure that generalizations are as convincing as possible.

Questions for Self Evaluation of Sampling Procedure

1. To define Population

(a) Have you defined the population or universe of your study?

(b) Have you fixed up the limits of the population in terms of geographical, demographic and relevant criteria?

(c) Can you say with full confidence that a particular unit or element belongs to your population?

(d) Have you an assured access to all elements of the population?

2. To Finalize the Sampling Frame

(a) Is the sampling frame available or can it be constructed easily?

(b) Have you checked and ensured that the sampling frame is up to data and correct and does not have any omissions or duplications?

(c) Have you made sure that the sampling frame does not exhibit any periodicity or other arrangements of elements?

(d) Have you given a serial order to the elements or listed them up?

(e) Does the sampling frame contain elements according to the sampling unit such as individuals or groups or books etc.?

(f) Have you decided on the sampling unit?

(g) Does your sampling unit coincide with the experimental unit or unit of data collection and analysis?

3. To decide Sample Size

(a) Have you decided upon the size of the sample you wish to have?

(b) Is it ensured that no personal judgment or intention has any place in the decision about the sample size?

(c) Is the decision of sample size based on some sound statistical considerations?

(d) Does the decision about sample size take care of the homogeneity or heterogeneity of the population?

(e) Have you decided upon the magnitude of the error or discrepancy acceptable to you in deciding about the size of the sample?

(f) Is your sample large enough to be adequate for the purpose of the study?

(g) Is your sample size large enough to be representative of the population?

4. To Select the Sampling Technique

(a) Are you using a probability sampling design?

(b) Have you specifically mentioned the randomization technique used in your study?

(c) Have you used tables of random numbers or some good mechanical device or computer services for the selection of the sample out of the serially arranged sampling frame?

(d) Did you stratify the population and obtain/prepare sampling frames for sub-populations?

(e) Are the criteria of stratification based on a sound evidence of the known relationship with the variables of the study?

(f) Did you check whether the stratification criteria had no known relationship between / among themselves? If yes, did you drop some of them?

(g) Are you giving proportional/optimal representation to all stratification criteria?

5

DATA COLLECTION

Primary Data Sources and Secondary Data Sources

The question of how a person can best gather and organize research data is probably a problem with every researcher. Extensive gathering and organizing of materials are very much necessary for the satisfactory completion of any research. Sources of data can be divided into Primary or Field sources and Secondary or the Documentary Sources. While the information given/collected by individuals and groups constitute the Primary Source. Books, manuscripts, diaries, letters, etc., form the Secondary Source.The difference between Primary and Secondary Data is a matter of relativity. Data which are primary in the hands of one become secondary in the hands of another. Data are primary for the individual agency and institution collecting them, whereas for the rest of the world they are secondary.

Sources of Data can be divided into Primary Sources and Secondary Sources:

Primary Sources

Primary sources of data can be considered as being of two types, the first of which consist of original works, based on a person's thoughts. A second type of primary source consists of data gathered at first hand and usually organized and presented by the person(s) who gathered them. (Mabry, 1999).

1. Questionnaire

Questionnaire is used to collect data directly from large groups of people with diverse characteristics. Questionnaire is either given personally to the informants or sent through mails. Generally, a questionnaire consists of several types of questions and scales. It should be suitable to the comprehensive level of the respondents. Characteristics of a good questionnaire are:

(a) To deal with a specific topic that the respondent will recognize as important enough to spend his time on;

(b) It seeks only that information that cannot be obtained from other sources;

(c) It is attractive and well arranged;

(d) It is as short as possible, only long enough to get the essential data;

(e) Each question deals with a single idea. All questions are worded as simple and clear as possible;

(f) The questions are objective, with no leading suggestions as to the responses desired;

(g) It is proceeded from general to specific responses; and

(h) It is easy to tabulate and interpret.

2. Interviews

Interview is an important technique in data collection. It is considered the best way/device of collecting data. It suits well to study the personality characteristics of individuals. Interviews are helpful to study the opinion, attitudes and values of people. Interviews are a purposeful conversation between the interviewer and respondents. It is intended for specific purposes and focused on some specific areas. Standardized interviews use schedules which are prepared after careful planning and discussion to get answers for the research problem.

3. Case Study

Case Study method is the intensive study of unexplored areas of human behaviors. It is concerned with the personal experiences of the individual and to understand the behavior patterns of a particular individual by getting the detailed account in depth. The focus is on individuals, situations, groups or communities.

Other examples of sources of primary data are Census data, verbatim of interviews, attitude and opinion surveys, and oral histories.

Of the limitations of primary data, Mabry, (1999) writes, "For a researcher to have a large amount of primary source material is akin to having a gold mine for she/he will have found a wealth of highly valuable information. At the same time, it should be noted that like any self-report, such materials are limited to what persons have been willing to share with others in either oral or written form. Original data gathered at first hand, such as through interviews, are also limited by the interests of the researchers who gathered the data in that their interest will have led them to ask certain kinds of questions but not others." Primary data are generally used in those areas and cases where the secondary data provide an adequate basis for analysis.

Secondary Sources

Secondary sources means data that are already available i.e., they refer to the data which have already been collected and analyzed by someone else. When the researcher utilizes secondary data, he has to look into various sources from where he can obtain them. In this case he is certainly not confronted with the problems that are usually associated with the collection of original data. Secondary data may either be published data or unpublished data.

Usually published data are available in:

(a) various publications of the central, state and local governments;

(b) various publications of foreign governments or of international bodies and their subsidiary organizations;

(c) technical and trade journals;

(d) books, magazines and newspapers;

(e) report and publications of various associations connected with business and industry, banks, stock exchanges, etc.

(f) reports prepared by research scholars, universities, economists, etc. in different fields, and

(g) public records and statistics, historical documents, and other sources of published information. (Raj, 2005)

Researcher must be very careful in using secondary data. He must make a minute scrutiny because it is just possible that the secondary data may be unsuitable or may be inadequate in the context of the problem which the researcher wants to study. By way of caution, the researcher, before using secondary data, must see that they possess the following characteristics:

1. **Reliability of Data:** The reliability can be tested by finding out such things about the said data: (a) Who collected the data? (b) What were the sources of data? (c)Were they collected by using proper methods? (d) At what time were they collected? (e) Was there any bias of the compiler? (f) What level of accuracy was desired and was it achieved?
2. **Suitability of Data:** The data that are suitable for one enquiry may not necessarily be found suitable in another enquiry. Hence, if the available data are found to be unsuitable, they should not be used by the researcher. In this context, the researcher must very carefully scrutinize the definition of various terms and units of collection used at the time of collecting the data from the primary source originally.
3. Similarly, the object, scope and nature of the original enquiry must also be studied. If the researcher finds differences in these, the data will remain unsuitable for the present enquiry and should not be used.
4. **Adequacy of Data**: If the level of accuracy achieved in data is found inadequate for the purpose of the present enquiry, they will be considered as inadequate and should not be used by the researcher. The data will also be considered inadequate if they are related to an area which may be either narrower or wider than the area of the present enquiry.

Working about the thought of other persons, or works based on data gathered by some one else for another purpose, are known as secondary sources. It is not always necessary to collect data from the field directly. The needed data may be got from the information, which were collected already for different purposes. Personal letters, diaries, log and other government documents, periodicals like census, reports health statistics, statistical records, etc. are secondary sources. This type of data is not considered inferior. Since these secondary data are readymade and time saving, they are commonly used in research. The contents of newspapers, magazines, books, journals, radio and television programs also provide a rich source of data.

Sometimes they are not found authentic and their accuracy and representation may be poor. "In most studies researchers will use both kinds of materials – consulting primary sources to gather materials which they consider relevant, and consulting secondary sources to see, among other things, how other researchers have interpreted the same materials", writes (Mabry, 1999).

Figure 5.1

SOURCES OF DATA

- Primary sources
  - (a) Questionnaire
  - (b) Interview
  - (c) Case Study
- Secondary Sources
  - Internal Source
  - External Source
    - Private Documents
      - (a) Life History
      - (b) Diaries
      - (c) Letters
    - Public Documents
      - Published Records
        - Memories, Journals & Magazines
        - Newspapers
        - Radio
        - T.V.
        - Films
        - Public Speeches
        - Internet
      - Unpublished Records

Internal Source and External Source

There are two categories of secondary data namely Internal

Secondary data and External Secondary data.

Internal data refers to information that already exists within the organization in which the research problem arises. External data refers to information which is collected by a source external to the organization (Saravanavel, 1999).

Classification of Documents

A document is anything in writing that contains the matter of sociological or other documents of importance. It includes written evidences such as life histories, diaries, letters, official and unofficial records, proceedings of parliaments, committees, courts, societies etc., business and legal papers, any act or constitution, official statistics, report of surveys, newspaper reports, editorials, speeches, pamphlets etc. A document may be published or unpublished. Documents have been classified as personal documents and public documents.

1. Private Documents

Private or personal documents are recorded by the individuals. Personal documents may be divided as life history, diary, letters, and memoirs:

(a) **Life History:** Life history contains all kinds of biographical materials.

(b) **Diaries:** People record their daily events of life and feelings and reaction to those events in diaries. Diaries are one of the most important sources of knowing the life history of a person.

(c) **Letters:** Letters are also a reliable material which throws light upon more intimate aspects of an event and also helps to understand the attitude of a person and the trend of his mind.

(d) **Memoirs:** People write memoirs of their travels, important events of life and other significant events which they come across.This also give useful material and information regarding the language, social customs, religious faiths, culture and many other aspects. Memoirs are different form of Diaries as the Memoirs describe only some events and are more elaborated than diaries.

2. Public Documents

Public Documents are different from Private Documents. Public Documents are divided into Unpublished Records and Published Records.

(a) **Unpublished Records**: They deal with the matters of public interest but not available to the public in the published form.

(b) **Published Records:** These are available to the public for investigation and perusal. Most of the published documents are considered reliable. Journals, magazines and newspapers provide very valuable contemporary information of latest events. Film, television, radio and public speeches also supply useful information about contemporary issues.

Advantages of Secondary Sources of Data

Secondary Sources of Data are claimed to have the following merits:

1. ***Provides an insight into Total Situations:*** The purpose of the use of available materials is to explore the nature of the data and the subjects to get an insight into the total situation. While looking for the data required by the researcher he may uncover many more available data than are often assumed to exist. Thus secondary data contributes significantly to the unfolding of hidden information.

2. ***Helps in the Formulation of Hypothesis:*** The use of Secondary sources of data helps in the formulation of research hypothesis. While a research writer may have one / two hypotheses which he might have deduced from theory, the study of secondary materials may suggest further hypotheses. If a research idea or hypothesis can be formulated in such a manner that the available recorded material bears on the question, the use of such material becomes possible.

3. ***Helps in Testing the Hypothesis:*** The available records may also help in testing the hypothesis.

4. ***Provides Supplementary Information:*** The available documents may be used to supplement or to check information gathered specifically for the purposes of a given investigation.

Disadvantages of Secondary Sources of Data

There are some disadvantages too for the secondary data:

1. Collected for Specific Purpose: Data are often collected with a specific purpose in mind, a purpose that may produce deliberate or unintentional bias. Thus, secondary sources must be evaluated carefully. The fact that secondary data were collected originally for particular purposes may produce other problems.Category definitions, particular measures or treatment effects may not be the most appropriate for the purpose at hand.

2. Old Data: Secondary data are by definition, old data. Thus, the data may not be particularly timely for older purposes.

3. Aggregation of Data in Inappropriate Unit: Seldom are secondary data available at the individual observation level. This means that the data are aggregated in some form, and the unit of aggregation may be inappropriate for a particular purpose.

Researchers use both kinds of sources, both primary and secondary, to gather material that are relevant to the field of research. Although primary source materials are a goldmine for researchers, such materials are limited to fulfill the requirements of the researcher. Secondary sources of data are increasingly available covering diverse fields and an investigator or researcher can find required data readily available to him in many cases.

While in many cases information availed through primary source will not have authentication, the sources from secondary sources are in most cases authenticated records and we can rely on them more depending upon the authority of the publication. In any case questions concerning the evaluation of data, such as the sources of data, measures used, the time of data collection, and the appropriateness of analyses and conclusions should be taken care of before taking the data for research. Information from Radio, T.V, Films, Public speeches, newspaper internet have only a secondary value in comparison with other published documents of appropriate authorities.

Methods of Collecting Data

The task of data collection begins after a research problem

has been defined and research design/plan chalked out. While deciding about the methods of data collection to be used for the study, the researcher should keep in mind two types of data, viz., primary and secondary. The primary data are those which are collected afresh and for the first time, and thus happen to be original in character. The secondary data, on the other hand, are those which have already been collected by someone else and which have already been passed through certain process. The researcher would have to decide which sort of data he would be using for his study and accordingly he will have to select one or the other method of data collection. The methods of collecting primary and secondary data differ since primary data are to be originally collected; while in case of secondary data the nature of data collection work is searching and that of compilation (Kothari, 1990).

Different Methods of Collecting Data

There are several methods of collecting primary data, particularly in surveys and descriptive research. Important ones are: (i) Observation method; (ii) Interview method; (iii) Through questionnaires; (iv) Through schedules and other methods.

Observation Method

The observation method is the most commonly used method specially in studies relating to behavioral science. Observation becomes a scientific tool and the method of data collection for the researcher when it serves a formulated research purpose; is systematically planned and recorded and is subjected to checks and controls on validity and reliability. Under the Observation method, the information is sought by way of investigator's own direct observation without seeking information form the respondent.

Advantages

1. The main advantage of this method is that subjective bias is eliminated, if observation is done accurately.
2. The information obtained under this method relates to what is currently happening; it is not complicated by either the past behavior or future intentions or attitudes.
3. This method is independent of respondents willingness to

respond and as such is relatively less demanding of active co-operation on the part of respondents as happens to be the case in the interview or the questionnaire method.

4. This method is suitable in studies which deal with respondents who are not capable of giving verbal reports of their feelings for one reason or the other.

Limitation

1. It is an expensive method.
2. The information obtained by this method is very limited.
3. Sometimes unforeseen factors may interfere with the observational task.
4. At times the fact that some people are rarely accessible to direct observation creates obstacle for this method to collect data effectively.

Different Types of Observation Method

1. ***Structured Observation:*** While using the observation method, the researcher should keep in mind things like: what should be observed? How the observations should be recorded? Or how the accuracy of observation can be ensured? In case the observation is characterized by a careful definition of the units to be observed, the style of recording the observation, standardized conditions of observation and the selection of pertinent data of observation are called 'structured observation'.
2. ***Unstructured Observation:*** When observation is to take place without these characteristics to be thought of in advance, the same is termed unstructured observation'. Structured observation is considered appropriate in descriptive studies, whereas in an exploratory study the observational procedure is most likely to be relatively unstructured.
3. ***Participant Observation:*** If the observer observes by making himself, more or less, a member of the group he is observing so that he can experience what the members of the group experience, the observation is called as the 'participant observation'

4. ***Non–participant Observation:*** When the observer observes without any attempt on his part to experience through participation what others feel, the observation of this type is often termed as 'Non-participant observation'.

5. ***Disguised observation:*** When the observer is observing in such a manner that his presence may be unknown to the people he is observing, such an observation is called as 'Disguised Observation'.

6. ***Controlled Observation:*** When observation takes place according to define pre-arranged plans, involving experimental procedures, the same is termed as 'Controlled observation'. In this case, precision instruments are used as aids to accuracy and standardization. Such observation has a tendency to supply formalized data upon which generalizations can be built with some degree of assurance.

7. ***Uncontrolled Observation:*** If the observation takes places in the natural setting, it is termed as 'uncontrolled observation'. In uncontrolled observation, no attempt is made to use precision instruments. The major aim of this type of observation is to get a spontaneous picture of life and persons. It has a tendency to supply naturalness and completeness of behavior, allowing sufficient time for observing it. The main disadvantage of non-controlled observation is that of subjective interpretation. There is also the danger of having the feeling that we know more about the observed phenomena than we actually do.

Interview Method

This method can be used through personal interviews and, if possible, through telephonic Interviews.

Personal Interview

Personal interview method requires a person known as the interviewer asking questions generally in a face-to-face contact with the other person or persons. (At times the interviewer may also ask certain questions and the interviewer responds to these, but usually the interviewer initiates the interview and collects information.) This sort of interview may be in the form of direct personal investigation or it may be an indirect oral investigation. In the case of direct personal investigation the interviewer has to collect the information personally from the sources concerned. He has to be on the spot and had to meet people from whom data have to be collected. This method is particularly suitable for intensive investigations. But in certain cases it may not be possible or worthwhile to contact directly the persons concerned or on account of the extensive scope of enquiry, the direct personal investigation technique may not be used. In such cases an indirect oral examination can be conducted under which the interviewer has to cross-examine other persons who are supposed to have knowledge about the problem under investigation and the information thus obtained is recorded. A tape recorder can be used at the time of personal interview for rechecking.

Different types of Personal Interview

1. ***Structured Interview:*** The method of collecting information through personal interviews is usually carried out in a structured way. Such interviews involve the use of a set of pre-determined questions and of highly standardized techniques of recording. Thus, the interviewer in a structured interview follows a rigid procedure laid down, asking questions in a form and order prescribed.

2. ***Unstructured Interview:*** Unstructured interviews are characterized by a flexibility of approach to questioning. This type of interviews do not follow a system of predetermined questions and standardized techniques of recording information. In a non–structured interview, the interviewer is allowed much greater freedom to ask in case of need, supplementary questions or at times he may omit certain questions if the situation so requires. He may even change the sequences of questions. He has relatively greater freedom while recording the responses to include some aspects and exclude others. But this sort of flexibility results in lack of comparability of one interview with another and the analysis of unstructured responses becomes much more difficult and time-consuming than of the structured responses obtained in case of structured interviews. Unstructured interviews

demand deep knowledge and greaterskill on the part of the interview. This kind of interview happens to be thecentral technique of collecting information in case of exploratory or formulative research studies. But in the case of descriptive studies, the technique of structured interview is often used because of its being more economical, providing a safe basis for generalization and requiring relatively lesser skill on the part of the interviewer.

3. ***Focused Interview:*** This is meant to focus attention on the given experience of the respondent and its effects. Under it the interviewer has the freedom to decide the manner and sequence in which the questions would be asked and has also the freedom to explore reasons and motives. The main task of the interviewer in case of a focused interview is to confine the respondent to a discussion of issues with which he seeks consensus. Such interviews are used generally in the development of hypotheses and constitute a major type of unstructured interviews.
4. ***Clinical Interview:*** This is concerned with broad underlying feelings or motivations or with the course of individual's life experience. The method of eliciting information under it is generally left to the interviewer's discretion.
5. ***Non-Directive Interview:*** In case of non-directive interview, the interviewer's function is simply to encourage the respondent to talk about the given topic with a bare minimum direct questioning. The interview often acts as a catalyst to a comprehensive expression of the respondent's feelings and beliefs and of the frame of reference within which such feelings and beliefs take on personal significance.

Merits and Demerits of Personal Interviews

Merits

1. More information in greater depth can be obtained.
2. Interviewer by his own skill can overcome the resistance, if any, of the respondents; the interview method can be made to yield and an almost perfect sample of the general population.

3. There is greater flexibility under this method as the opportunity to restructure questions is always there, specially in case of unstructured interviews.
4. Observation method can as well be applied to recording verbal answers to various questions.
5. Personal information can as well be obtained easily under this method.
6. Samples can be controlled more effectively as there arises no difficulty of the missing returns; non-response generally remains very low.
7. The interviewer can usually control which person(s) will answer the questions.This is not possible in mailed questionnaire approach. If so desired, group discussions may also be held.
8. The interviewer may catch the informant off-guard and thus may secure the most spontaneous reactions that would be the case if a mailed questionnaire is used.
9. The language of the interview can be adapted to the ability or educational level of the person interviewed and as such misinterpretations concerning questions can be avoided.
10. The interviewer can collect supplementary information about the respondent's personal characteristics and environment which is often of great value in interpreting results.

Demerits

1. It is a very expensive method, specially when large and widely spread geographical sample is taken.
2. There remains the possibility of the bias of the interviewer as well as that of the respondent; there also remains the headache of supervision and control of interviewers.
3. Certain types of respondents such as important officials or executives or people in high income groups may not be easily approachable under this method and to that extent the data may prove inadequate.
4. The method is relatively more time-consuming, specially when

the sample is large and re-calls upon the respondents are necessary.

5. The presence of the interviewer on the spot may over-stimulate the respondent, sometimes even to the extent that he may give imaginary information just to make the interview interesting.
6. Under the interview method the organization required for selecting, training and supervising the field staff is more complex with formidable problems.
7. Interviewing at times may also introduce systematic errors.
8. Effective interview presupposes proper rapport with respondents that would facilitate free and frank responses. This is often a very difficult requirement.

Telephonic Interview

This method of collecting information concerns with contacting respondents on telephone itself. It is not a very widely used method, but plays an important part in industrial surveys, particularly in developed regions. The chief merits and demerits of such a method are:

Merits

1. It is more flexible in comparison to mailing method.
2. It is faster than other methods, i.e., a quick way of obtaining information.
3. It is cheaper than personal interviewing method.
4. Recall is easy; call backs are simple and economical.
5. There is a higher rate of response than what we have in mailing method; the non-response is generally very low.
6. Replies can be recorded without causing embarrassment to respondents.
7. Interviewer can explain requirements more easily.
8. At times, access can be gained to respondents who otherwise cannot be contacted for one reason or the other.
9. No field staff is required.

10. Representative and wider distribution of sample is possible.

Demerits

1. Little time is given to respondents for considered answers; interview period is not likely to exceed five minutes in most cases.
2. Survey is restricted to respondents who have telephone and mobile facilities.
3. Extensive geographical coverage may get restricted by cost considerations.
4. It is not suitable for intensive surveys where comprehensive answers are required to various questions.
5. Possibility of the bias of the interviewer is relatively more.
6. Questions have to be short and to the point; probes are difficult to handle.

Collection of Data through Questionnaire

This method of data collection is quite popular particularly in case of big enquiries. It is being adopted by private individuals, research workers, private and public organizations and even by governments. In this method a questionnaire is sent to the persons concerned with a request to answer the questions and return the questionnaire. A questionnaire consists of a number of questions printed or typed in a definite order on a form or set of forms to be answered by the respondents.

Merits

1. There is low cost even when the participants in this proceeds is spread over a wide geographical area.
2. It is free from the bias of the interviewer; answers are in respondent's own words.
3. Respondents have adequate time to give well thought out answers.
4. Respondents who are not easily approachable can also be reached conveniently.
5. Large samples can be made use of and thus the results can be made more dependable and reliable.

Demerits

1. Low rate of return of the duly filled in questionnaires; bias due to non-response is often indeterminate.
2. It can be used only when respondents are educated and cooperating.
3. The control over questionnaire may be lost once it is sent.
4. There is inbuilt inflexibility because of the difficulty of amending the approach once questionnaires have been dispatched.
5. There is also the possibility of ambiguous replies or omission of replies altogether to certain questions; interpretation of omissions is difficult.
6. It is difficult to know whether willing respondents are truly representative.
7. This method is likely to be the slowest of all.
(Kothari, 1999)

Main Aspects of a Questionnaire

Quite often questionnaire is considered as the heart of a survey operation. Hence it should be very carefully constructed. If it is not properly set up, then the survey is bound to fail. This fact requires us to study the main aspects of a questionnaire, viz., the general form, question sequence and question formulation and wording.

1. **General Form**

   So far as the general form of questionnaire is concerned, it can either be structured or unstructured questionnaire. Structured questionnaires are those in which there are definite, concrete and pre- determined questions. The questions are presented with exactly the same wording and in the same order to all respondents. Resort is taken to this sort of standardization to ensure that all respondents reply to the same set of questions. The form of the question may be either closed (i.e., of the type 'yes' or 'no') or open (i.e., inviting free response) but should be stated in advance and not constructed during questioning.

2. Structured Questionnaires

Structured Questionnaires may also have fixed alternative questions in which responses of the informants are limited to the stated alternatives. Thus a highly structured questionnaire is one in which all questions and answers are specified and comments in the respondent's own words are held to the minimum. When these characteristics are not present in a questionnaire, it can be termed as unstructured questionnaire. More specifically we can say that in an unstructured questionnaire, the interviewer is provided with a general guide on the type of information to be obtained, but the exact question formulation is largely his own responsibility and replies are to be taken down in the respondent's own words to the extent possible; in some situations tape recorders may be used to achieve this goal.

3. Qr stions Sequence

In order to make the questionnaire effective and to ensure quality of the replies received, a researcher should pay attention to the question-sequence in preparing the questionnaire. A proper sequence of questions reduces considerably the chances of individual questions being misunderstood. The question–sequence must be clear and smoothly-moving, meaning thereby that the relation of one question to another should be readily apparent to the respondent, with questions that are easiest to answer being put in the beginning. The first few questions are particularly important because they are likely to influence the attitude of the respondent and in seeking his desired cooperation. The opening questions should be such as to arouse human interest.

The following type of questions should generally be avoided as opening questions.

- Questions that put too much strain on the memory or intellect of the respondent;
- Questions of a personal character;
- Questions related to personal wealth, etc.

Question Formulation and Wording

With regard to this aspect of questionnaire, the researcher should note that each question must be very clear for any sort of misunderstanding otherwise it can do irreparable harm to a survey. Questions should also be impartial in order not to give a biased picture of the true state of affairs. Questions should be constructed with a view to their forming a logical part of a well thought out tabulation plan.

In general, all questions should meet the following standards:

- should be easily understood;
- should be simple, i.e., should convey only one thought at a time;
- should be concrete and should conform as much as possible to the respondent's way of thinking to enable him to answer easily.

Collection of Data through Schedules

This method of data collection is very much like the collection of data through questionnaire, with little difference which lies in the fact that schedules (proforma containing a set of questions) are being filled in by the enumerators who are specially appointed for the purpose. These enumerators along with schedules, go to respondents, put to them the questions from the proforma, in the order of questions which are listed and record the replies in the space meant for the same in the proforma.In certain situations, schedules may be handed over to respondents and enumerators may help them in recording their answers to various questions in the said schedules. Enumerators explain the aims and objects of the investigation and also remove the difficulties which any respondent may feel in understanding the implications of a particular question or the definition or concept of difficult terms.

This method requires the selection of enumerators for filling up schedules or assisting respondents to fill up schedules and as such enumerators should be very carefully selected. The enumerators should be trained to perform their job well and the nature and scope of the investigation should be explained to them thoroughly so that they may well understand the implications of different questions put in the schedule. Enumerators should be intelligent and must possess the capacity of cross-examination in order to find out the truth. Above all, they should be honest, sincere, hardworking and should have patience and perseverance. This method is very useful in extensive enquiries and can lead to fairly reliable results. It is, however, very expensive and is usually adopted in investigations conducted by governmental agencies or by some big organizations. Population census all over the world is conducted through this method. (Kothari, 1999)

Types of Schedules

1. Observation Schedule

It offers the opportunity to uniform classification in recording the activities and social situations of persons or groups being observed. One observer and several others maybe employed to secure and uniform a systematic data.

An observation schedule serves the following purposes

(a) It is specific memory sticker

(b) It is an objective recording device

(c) It is a standardizing device

(d) It aids to delineate the scope of the study

2. Document Schedule

These are used for recording data obtained from documents, case histories and other materials. In order to secure measurable data, the items included on this type of form are limited. For example, study of criminal records might include such items as type of previous offence, age at time started to work, amount of education etc.

3. Evaluation Schedule

Schedules of this type are used to visualize the problems faced by or inherent in a given type of institution. The length of such inquiries depends upon the aspects of the given situation under investigation. The best example for such a schedule is "Census Schedule."

Essentials of a Good Schedule

According to Young (1975) there are two essential conditions of a good schedule. (1) Accurate communication and (2) Accurate response.

The following points are to be taken into account while preparing a schedule:

1. Paper
2. Size of schedule (Generally small size is preferable because it is handy, the most popular size is 81"/2x11")
3. Margin (A margin of ¾" on one side and nearly 1/5" or 1/6" on the other side should be left out),
4. Spacing
5. Printing and
6. Use of pictures

The whole schedule may be divided into three parts according to the nature of contents.

Introductory Part

Under this part, the items included are

1. Name and heading of the survey,
2. Serial or Case No.
3. General information about interview,
4. Place of interview and
5. Date and Time of interview.

Pre-testing and Checking Schedule

The questions which do not get consistent or definite responses should be revised in order to avoid errors. After the interviewers have read the interview schedule with care, the researcher should go over the schedule slowly and thoroughly with them, providing instructions and explanation as he goes along. After the explanation, the interviewers are asked to practice interviewing in pairs. Each interviewer is asked to go out and conduct three or four practiced interviews. Interviewers must be honest and interested in the topic of research. They are to perform interviews efficiently. They are expected to provide clear statements, including explanation of questions, probe to obtain the proper responses and record responses accurately.

Main Schedule

It is the most vital part and has to be prepared with great care, the schedule consists of questions as well as blank tables where information to be supplied by the informant has to be filled.

Instructions to Interviewers

This part consists of instructions or guidelines to be followed by the researchers in gathering information form the respondents.

Types of Questions

There are mainly nine different types of questions.

1. Number (value) question

A number question is a question in which the answer is not transformed into code, because the answer itself can be coded the same way as it has been recorded on the questionnaire at interview time. Questions of this type are related to age, number of children etc.

2. Structured questions

When answer to a question has been pre-conceived and classified into possible groups, it is known as a structured question.

For example: (a) Are your educated/ Uneducated (b) Are you Married/ Unmarried

3. Dichotomous Questions or Fixed Alternative Questions

When reply to a question is given in one of the two alternatives, the question is called dichotomous.

For example: Sex of the informant: Male/ Female.

4. Open-ended Questions

These questions generally relate to opinion sought about any particular Problem or suggestion invited about it.

For example: What do you think, are the main causes of present indiscipline among the students? What suggestions you offer to remove them?

5. Semi-Open-Ended Questions

These questions have a fixed number of alternatives plus an 'others' option. Questions of this type are: What do you suggest to remove indiscipline?

For example: (1) Suspension. (2) Dismissal or any other measure. (Specify)

6. Multiple Choice Questions

It is the opposite form of dichotomous questions. In these questions, the reply is not confined to two alternatives only, but may be one among the number of possible replies.

For example: What type of career do you propose to choose? (a) Business, (b) Industry, (c) Government Service, (d) Private Services (e) any other (specify).

7. Leading Questions

When reply to a question is suggested in a particular direction, it is known as leading, suggestive or directive question.

For Example: Do you think that education in municipal primary schools makes the children ill-mannered?

8. Ranking Item Questions

The multiple choice questions may also contain a number of alternatives. The only difference between these two is that whereas in the case of multiple choice questions, only one of the given answer is to be selected, in case of ranking item questions, order of preference is to be given for all.

For example: What is your preference to the following population control measures?

(a) Tubectomy (b) Vasectomy (c) Oral Pills (d) Contraceptives

Difference between Questionnaires and Schedules

Both questionnaires and schedules are popularly used as methods of collecting data in research surveys. There is much resemblance in the nature of these two methods and this fact has made many people to remark that from a practical point of view, the two methods can be taken to be the same. But from the technical point of view there are differences between the two. The important points of difference are as under:

1. The questionnaire is sent by post, without further assistance form the sender. The schedule is generally filled in by the research worker or the enumerator, who can explain questions when necessary.
2. Data collection through questionnaire method is relatively cheap. To collect data through schedules is relatively more expensive, due to involvement of enumerators and their training.
3. Non-response is usually high in case of questionnaires, as many people do not respond. Bias due to non-response often remains indeterminate. Non-response in case of schedules is very low because these are filled by research workers who are able to get answers to all questions. However, there is the possibility of interviewer bias and cheating.
4. In case of questionnaire, it is not always clear as to who replies, but in case of schedule the identity of the respondent is known.
5. The questionnaire method is likely to be very slow since respondents do not return the filled in questionnaire in time, but in case of schedules the information is collected instantly by the enumerators.
6. Personal contact is generally not possible in case of the questionnaire method, but in case of schedules direct personal contact is established with the respondents.
7. Questionnaire method can be used only when respondents are literates and cooperative, but in case of schedules the information can be gathered even when the respondents are illiterates.
8. Wider and more representative distribution of sample is possible under the questionnaire method, but in respect of schedules there usually remains the difficulty in sending enumerators to a wider area.
9. Risk of collecting incomplete and wrong information is relatively more under the questionnaire method, particularly when people are unable to understand the questions properly.

In case of schedules the information collected is generally complete and accurate as enumerators can remove the difficulties, if any, faced by respondents in correctly understanding the questions.

10. The success of the questionnaire method lies more on the quality of the questionnaire itself, but in the case of schedules much depends upon the honesty and competence of enumerators.
11. In order to attract the attention of respondents, the physical appearance of the questionnaire must be quite attractive, but this may not be so in case of schedules as they are to be filled in by the enumerators.
12. Along with schedules, observation method can also be used but such a thing is not possible while collecting data through questionnaires.

Case Study Method

Case study is basically the method of exploring and analyzing the life of a social unit be that a person, a family or an institution, or a community. In this method, various aspects of this unit are deeply and thoroughly studied, taking into account its past, present and future. Behavior patterns of a unit and its relationship with the environments is studied from all dimensions. It is a method which deals with processes that take place and their relationship. Its object is to locate factors that account for the behaviour pattern of a given unit. It is a form of qualitative analysis in which efforts are made to study in detail each and every aspect of a given unit (Young, 1960).

Characteristics of Case Study Method

Like every other method in social research, case study method has some important characteristics which are briefly discussed below:

1. First important characteristic of this method is that the social unit which is picked up for study is comprehensively studied in all its entirety. All aspects are deeply and thoroughly studied. Various factors which act or interact on that unit are carefully studied. In this study, both qualitative as well as quantitative aspects are given full weight and full consideration is given

to family, group and community life of the individual, group or even of the community as a whole.

2. In this method, approach of study is direct and neither abstract nor indirect.
3. Another characteristic of this method is that it studies both 'what and why'. In the first instance the researcher tries to describe complete behavioral patterns of a unit. After that has been done, his next attempt is to discover such factors which will rationally account for the behavior of the unit in social surroundings and set-up.
4. In this method the whole approach is not quantitative but qualitative. The idea is not merely to collect information but to go deep into the life of the unit concerned.
5. In this method the researcher can pick up for his study only one social unit. While studying effort, is made to know the mutual interrelationship of several factors.
6. This method tries to organize the individual unit into an integrated whole, in a manner that its integrity and wholesomeness can be preserved.In this all unifying bonds are created so that diverse elements are brought together in a well knit unit system. In this system individual, family, institution or group is considered as a unified whole.

Merits of Case Study Method

1. ***It helps in the Formulation of hypothesis:*** Every researcher, before finalizing his hypothesis and questionnaire tries to have proper analysis of many cases which center around his major problem. Preliminary study of the process is greatly facilitated by case documents, incorporating the pertinent data which will guide the later stages of research.

2. ***Intensive Study Possible:*** With the help of this method, it becomes possible to intensively study a unit from all aspects and thus to have deep probing, which is very essential for research work.

3. ***Helps in Understanding Behavior Pattern:*** One more advantage of this method is that being an exhaustive study, this method enables the researcher to understanding behavior pattern of the concerned unit directly and he can obtain information about inner strings of the person concerned.

4. ***No need of Sampling:*** Sampling involves many serious problems. Usually there is a complaint that some biases and personal prejudices have found entry in the sample. It is a method in which there is no need to pick up any sample and as such all the defects of sampling method do not get introduced in this method of study.

5. ***Study of Subjective Aspects:*** This method lays stress on the psychology of the person concerned, behavior of the individual, circumstances in which he placed himself and his reaction to certain situations of life and so on. It is with the help of the study that subjective aspects can be studied as thoroughly as possible.

6. ***Helps Studying Social Changes:*** Case study method also helps in studying social changes by thoroughly studying different facets of social units and changes which came with the passing of time by making certain inferences. It is an important method for understanding the past of a social unit and suggest measures for improvement in the present context.

7. ***Helps in Removing Defects of Research:*** It is a method in which some case studies are carried out in the first instance. It then becomes possible to find out, locate and identify possible defects which may creep in a full-scale study. In this way this method helps in removing many defects of a full-fledged study.

8. ***Help in Comparative Study:*** With the help of this method, two different sets of cases can be picked up and compared. Though in actual practice it is not possible to pick up two types of cases but once that has been done, it becomes easy to compare the two and as such comparative study becomes both easy as well as possible.

9. ***Increases Knowledge:*** When a researcher or an investigator studies all aspects of a social unit, both past, present and likely future and no aspect of the problem is left out, then his knowledge helps both in that particular study, as well as in all his subsequent research work. In this way, this method provides a very good training ground for social science researchers.

Limitations of Case Study Method

1. ***Danger of Subjectivity:*** In this method of study there is every danger of subjectivity because in it there is too much association of researcher with the social unit under study. The greater the rapport, the more subjective becomes the whole study. The subject is more likely to be self-justificatory than factual.

2. *Comparison not possible:* In social research, the investigation is to deal with human beings. They are quite different from each other. Their values, attitudes, behaviors, reactions, circumstances, etc. widely differ from each other. Accordingly it is very difficult to find out two identical cases. As such it is not possible to compare two case studies, because no two case studies can be similar.

3. *False Sense of Prestige:* The researcher comes to feel a false sense of certainty about his own conclusions. The danger, then, does not lie in any technical weakness of the approach to social processes or individual as a whole. The result of the certainty is that there is temptation to ignore basic principles of research designs. Since the researcher feels so very certain about the area of experience he is investigating, therefore, he feels no need to check the over-all design of study.

4. *No Method of Checking:* In this method, an investigator is assigned the responsibility of preparing the case history and study a particular case. He collects some information with some labor and provides that to the society. But there is no method of checking the information because no other investigator is working on the same or similar case. Thus, whatever information is supplied by the researcher that must be accepted and that is not healthy for an objective research.

5. *It is Time-Consuming:* The investigator is to study the case from all aspects and also its past, present and likely future. Not only this, but his behaviors, approaches and attitudes on the one hand and the circumstances on the other are required to be studied. The whole study is, therefore, very time consuming and only few researchers canle afforded.

6. *Ad-hocism:* It is a method in which there is maximum ad hocism. There is no method of picking up the case. It is left to the individual researcher to pick up a case of his choice without any criteria and to study that. There is no method of picking up the case as well. But in research, ad hocism does not work. Who knows that the case picked up for study is one which should or should not be studied or that the choice is right or wrong.

7. ***Possibility of Wrong Conclusions:*** In this method the investigator tries to arrive at certain conclusions on the basis of a case study. But it is always possible that the conclusions drawn on the basis of one case study may be wrong. In this way the researcher may draw wrong conclusions to the disadvantage of the society as a whole (Saravanavel, 2005).

8. ***Reliability of Source Material:*** Case study is prepared with the help of diaries, memories and personal papers and records of the persons concerned. Usually when a person records his life events, he does not give a true picture and considerable coloring is added. Usually more stress is laid on strong and bright side, whereas weak side is either concealed or underestimated and in many cases even side-lined and ignored. It is more or less impossible to remove colors from the events with the result that the conclusions drawn are a colored one and thus undependable.

9. ***False Generalization:*** In case study, only one social unit is studied and on the basis of conclusions drawn, efforts are made to derive certain general conclusions, which is not good for the society, particularly when no set rules are followed in case studies.

10. ***Too much Dependence on Memory:*** In a case study, the individual's case history is prepared by interviewing him and asking him questions about his past, circumstances in which he behaved in a particular manner and so on. In this way he is required to lay too much stress on his memory. There is every chance that the memory may fail him and he may not give true information or he may not be remembering an incident.

11. ***Time Gap:*** In a case study, if the individual is a social unit and he is asked to justify his past actions, there is every possibility that the information supplied may be undependable because of time gap between actual time of action and the time at which he is being questioned. Obviously he will need sufficient time to think, to justify his action according to changing situations and social considerations and so on, but a social researcher cannot afford long waiting.

12. ***Not possible to use it in Big Societies:*** One more limitation of this method is that this method can be used only in a limited way in small societies. It is not possible to use it in a big society.

13. ***Tendency to give Easy Answers:*** Usually when a person is approached by a researcher to give information about certain events with which he has been closely associated, he picks up the easiest way of answering the question, so that time is saved and there is no involvement in the controversy. He will therefore prefer to be very brief in giving answers or will simply avoid the researcher by saying, "I do not remember" or "I do not know" and so on. This tendency becomes more when the researcher is a stranger and the social unit does not know him. (Saravanavel, 2005)

Survey Method

One of the common methods of diagnosing and solving of social problems is that of undertaking surveys.

Definition and Scope of Social Survey

Dictionary meaning of survey is 'to overlook' and as such social survey implies identifying social problems. Many research problems required a systematic collection of data from population through the use of personal interview or other data gathering devices. These studies are usually called surveys, especially when they are concerned with large and widely diverse groups of people.

Kinds of Social Survey

Social surveys can be of different kinds. Its scope can be both very limited as well as very comprehensive. There are many kinds of survey, such as:

Regular or Ad hoc Survey

When a body/individual/ organization conducts some survey at regular intervals, e.g., Economic Survey of Reserve Bank of India, that is called a Regular Survey. On the other hand, when the survey is conducted with a view to finding out some information required for a particular purpose and the purpose of the survey is over as soon as the object is achieved, the survey is called an Ad hoc Survey.

Official and Non-official Survey

A survey can be conducted by the government for finding out

certain facts for official as well as for some philanthropic purposes. Such a survey is called official survey. Surveys are also conducted both by individuals as well as social and research organizations with or without the help of the government. Such surveys are called unofficial surveys.

Direct of Indirect Survey

Where the survey facts can be quantitatively interpreted, such surveys are called direct surveys. In case of indirect surveys, facts cannot be interpreted and results are to be concluded from the available data by some indirect methods.

Personal or Postal Survey

Personal Survey is one in which the surveyor himself is required to move about and collect information personally, but in the case of Postal Survey, the researcher gets information through post, i.e., by way of mailing some questionnaire.

Primary or Secondary Survey

Primary Survey is one in which the surveyor himself starts work on a particular subject and personally collects all data. In the case of Secondary Data, the surveyor himself does not start work but depends on the work which has already been done by somebody else. Obviously primary data is more important and dependable than the secondary data.

First or Repetitive Survey

When survey is carried out in a particular area or subject for the first time, it is called first or initial survey. When that is being carried out again and again, it is called Repetitive survey. In an initial survey more time and labor is required than on the repetitive survey.

Open or Confidential Survey

When the nature, purpose and result of survey are open to the public, it is called open or public survey. When the results of survey are only for the consumption of the body or organization which is carrying out survey, that can be called confidential survey.

Comprehensive or Limited Survey

When the survey covers a vast field and the survey questionnaire asks for information which is of a wide variety and range, the survey is called 'a comprehensive survey'. When the field covered is comparatively limited, it is called 'a limited survey'.

Advantages of Social Survey

Social surveys are really time-consuming and costly and as such these should be conducted with clear objective and carefulness. Some advantages of social survey are:

1. It is with the help of survey that it becomes possible to thoroughly and deeply study a problem in all aspect. It is only then that the causes of the problem can be studied and solution to be problem can be found out.
2. It is very useful to administrators and policy makers. Important legislative measures can be taken based on the findings of social surveys.
3. With the help of social surveys, the trends of changes in the society can be found out.
4. In a social survey, the researcher personally collects information; therefore, the data collected are based on the reality of life and circumstances. Thus the information collected is important and dependable.
5. In social surveys, many surveyors are sent to the field, and therefore the information collected and when compiled can be with no or minimum bias.
6. In every society there are many hidden factors which come to light only through field surveys which otherwise do not come to light because of vested interests of individuals or bodies. Community welfare can thus be ensured through social survey.
7. Another advantage is that with its help comparative study becomes possible. If comparative studies are available, the society on the whole gains.

Limitations of Social Survey

Social survey method of study has its own limitations as well as which are equally serious. Some of them are:

1. One limitation is of raising resources, both human and

financial. Heavy amounts and manpower in the form of trained investigators, field workers, researchers and so on are needed to conduct the survey which usually is not possible.

2. Another difficulty is that there can be no uniformity in data collection. When so many surveyors are in the field to collect data, there is every possibility that each one will give his own interpretation to the terms used in the data collection schedule. When there is no uniformity, there is bound to be some variance. There is also possibility of high rate of bias.
3. It is very time consuming. If efforts are made to complete the survey in a hurry, then their is the possibility of losing much of the needed information and thus the whole survey will be undependable.
4. When large scale surveys are undertaken, many unanticipated difficulties come up on the way which may hinder the progress. Some times the survey would seriously suffer to the state of even canceling the entire work.
5. Data collected with the help of survey method can be dependable only when two basic conditions are met. Firstly, the investigators who are given the responsibility of collecting data should be trained and persons with integrity, who realize their duty and responsibility; secondly the respondents should be prepared to cooperate and come out with correct information. Both these are serious hurdles.
6. Still another limitation is that if the survey of a particular local area is conducted, then obviously the results obtained will be applicable to that particular area and cannot be generalized. If the survey is spread over a vast area then the results become too general and focus of the study gets lost and thus is not of much use.
7. Usually large scale surveys cannot be undertaken and a way out of that which has been found out is to pick samples for the study. When sampling method is used then sampling errors are bound to creep in. In this all the defects of sampling method of social research get introduced in the study. (Wilkinson & Shaudarkar, 1994)

Case study method has its own limitations but these days this method is being increasingly used because of tremendous improvements in the techniques of these studies. Because of these new trends data are amendable to quantification and statistical treatment. These have been found almost unavoidable for therapeutic and administrative purposes and the matter collected through case studies are found useful for basic research. Survey method these days has been found quite useful and is being extensively used both by governmental and non-governmental agencies. Limited as well as comprehensive surveys are being quite commonly conducted. Business houses as well as political parties use this method to serve their purpose. Social surveys go a long way in so far as social planning is concerned. In a country like India where social problems are really very serious, social planning and social survey will go a long way in solving many of our social problems.

6

THREE GUIDING PRINCIPLES IN RESEARCH

Pilot Study

Meaning of Pilot Study

After the literature has been carefully studied and experts consulted, the researcher may still have only a vague idea of what are the crucial elements in his problem. A pilot study, or survey as sometimes called, may then be launched as a step preliminary to the formulation of a schedule. Pilot study is a preliminary study conducted on a limited scale before the original studies are carried out in order to gain some primary information, on the basis of which the main project would be planned and formulated. The preliminary survey or study of the universe in question helps to acquire a general knowledge about the problem which ultimately helps to know the nature and different aspects of the problem.

Need for Pilot Study

The pilot study is undertaken without formulating any hypothesis about the problem. It is made on a small sample, but it is necessary that the individuals of the sample should form the actual group to be studied. That is, they should be respondents who would act as representatives of the entire groups of respondents. At this stage all that can be formulated is an interview guide. Thus the researcher studies the field in a very nondirective fashion. The questions are structured very little and controlled only by dealing with these general areas which he has reason to think are important. During this kind of flexible interviewing, he tries to follow up every promising lead which may appear, as to meaning of phrases, embarrassing areas of inquiry, differences of response to what seems to be the same question, new areas of subject matter, etc., The researcher, then, is not putting neat hypotheses for a subject to the test at this stage but is clarifying and formulating hypotheses for a subsequent study. Not only is he uncertain as the materials he wants to inquire about, but he may even be uncertain as to whom he wishes to interview. This stage does not usually warrant a formal sample design, but the investigator must be sure that he interviews a wide variety of the various types making up the final sample to be studied. Further, he must be alert to field sampling problems which may warn him to take precautions at the stage of formal sample design. The results of these "intensive interview" must then be written up and carefully analyzed, for they furnish the logical basis upon which the subsequent questionnaire will be based. If well done and thoroughly exploited, the pilot study will usually prove to be substantial saver of time and effort by helping to avoid erroneous and insignificant hypotheses, (Saravanavel, 1999).

Advantages of Pilot Study

Following are the advantages of the pilot study:

1. Pilot study will permit a preliminary testing of the hypotheses and lead to testing of more precise hypotheses in the main study. It may lead to change some hypotheses, drop some, and bring in new ones.
2. It often provides the research worker with ideas, approaches, and clues, not foreseen prior to the pilot study.
3. It helps to make the needed alterations that may be useful in the data collecting methods.
4. It greatly reduces the number of treatment errors, because unforeseen problems revealed in the pilot study may be overcome in redesigning the main body.
5. It may save the research worker a major expenditure of time and money on a research project that will yield nothing. The pilot study usually provides enough data for the research worker to make a sound decision on the advisability of going ahead with the main study.
6. In the pilot study, the researcher may try out a number of alternative measures, and then select those that produce the best results for the main study. If a student plans to continue

beyond the Master's degree, his Master's research may lead to his Doctoral research, (Borg. 1963).

Role of Pilot Study in Identifying the Variables Involved in Research

Pilot study enables the researcher to gain some systematic knowledge of the universe and its population, on which would be based the main or principal study. The former plays a very vital role in identifying the various variables involved in research, the nature of the problem, the nature of the respondents, possible difficulties in the procedure of interview, kind of response that are likely to be available, etc. On the basis of the information gathered or experience gained during such a study, the schedule/questionnaire prepared after such a study shall be more or less foolproof and the environment of research is clearer to the researcher. For example, if the problem is the study of women executives of a particular region, a small group of women executives from this region is chosen and their problems enquired into by interview. This preliminary study would go a long way in formulating the schedule; many a time certain facts undreamt of by the researcher come to surface. Informal techniques will remain invaluable at the pilot study of even formal surveys, to provide guidance on what are the important questions and how they should be asked. A pilot study is a standard practice with professional survey bodies and is widely used in research surveys.

Pilot study specifically provides the following:

1. The adequacy of the sampling frame from which it is proposed to select the sample.
2. The variability (with regard to the subject under investigation) within the population to be surveyed).
3. The non–response/non contacts rate to be expected.
4. The suitability of the method of collecting the data.
5. The adequacy of the questionnaire, accuracy, efficiency and clarity, the kind of interviewers and respondent.
6. The efficiency of the instructions and general briefing of interviewers.
7. The code chosen for pre-coded questions i.e., to decide upon the alternative answers to be answered for in the coding.

8. The probable cost and duration of the main survey and of its various stages – suggesting where economics can be made/ the cost data will also have a bearing on the sample design. and
9. The efficiency of the organization in the field, in the office, and in the communication between the two (Claus and Kalton, 1976).

The pilot study will certainly help to clarify many of the problems left unsolved by the previous tests, but it will not necessarily throw up all the troubles of the main study. Much bigger scale of this is almost a guarantee of snags and headaches of which the pilot study gave no warning. The size and design of the pilot study is a matter of convenience, time and money. It should be large enough to fulfill the above functions, and the sample should ideally be of a comparable structure to that of the main study; in practice it is rarely feasible for it to be as widespread as the main sample.

Once the pilot study is over, the researcher should ask himself, whether in the light of its tests, the main study is still worth carrying out as planned. There are cases in which an intelligent reading of the pilot study evidence would lead him to take a more suitable view of the main study's potentialities; to see that some of the objectives are not worth pursuing if people are unwilling or unable to give accurate information; and to realize that he cannot cover as wide a field of enquiry or population as planned.The pilot study is thus the researcher's last safeguard against the possibility that the main study may be effective.

Significance of Pilot Study

1. Helps in the Respondent Selection Procedure

It helps in bringing out the inadequacies of the draft questionnaire. It throws light on several difficult, ambiguous, partial, irrelevant and 'do not know' questions and provides clues of dealing with them. It also provides an estimate about the non-response rate and the reasons thereof, success rate by number of call-backs, best time of the day or day of the week for interviewing, characteristics of unavailable respondents and the improvements which should be made in the respondent selection procedure.

2. Provides Training and Motivation to Interviewers

It unfolds how effective the training has been in ridding the interviewers of their prejudices and in motivating them, what are the deficiencies of training curricula, staff incentives, etc.

3. Inculcates Seriousness and Honesty to Interviewers

It helps in distinguishing the serious type of interviewers from the non-serious and honest from the cheat. It also helps in finding out the type of person 'most likely' to be a good interviewer in the study.

4. Provides Opportunities to Learn About Local Culture and Build Self Confidence

It allays interviewers' fears about overtly sensitive questions and builds their self-confidence. They learn a variety of tactics and codes of conduct which they should follow to build rapport with the respondents. They also learn to respect the local culture.

5. Provides a Trial or Rehearsal to Test Interviewers' Work

It tests interviewers' stamina to work under conditions of personal discomfort, stress and fatigue.

6. Improves the Efficiency of the Survey Organization

It tests the efficiency of the survey organization in the field, in the office and in the communication between the two. It shows how much and what type of supervision is needed and how can the instructions be made more effective. In other words, what should be the supervisor to interviewer ratio, frequencies of supervisory contact and so on.

7. Identifies the Needs of Tools and Equipments for Survey

It helps in identifying the needs for different kinds of equipments and vehicles. Conditions for local terrain will decide the need for different types of transport. Similarly the climate of the region will decide the need for different field equipments which may range from a rain coat and mosquito net to be rolled, cooking pots and lanterns. Depending on the nature of the problem, the interviewers may also need official letters of introduction, badges or sanction to proceed with their work.

8. Facilitates to Estimate the Project Cost and Time

It provides data for making estimates of time and cost for completing various phases of the project and shows ways to effect savings.

In summary, a pilot study helps in selecting a respondent, provides training and motivation to interviewers, inculcates in them seriousness and honesty, provides opportunities to learn local culture and thereby build self confidence, provides time for rehearsal, improves efficiency of the survey organization. Also it identifies the needs of tools and equipment required for the survey and facilitates to estimate the project cost and time. (Saravanavel, 2005)

Ethical Issues in Research / Research Ethics

Research ethics, refers to the application of moral standards to determine decisions at the level of planning, research design, operationalization of concepts to measure variables, analyzing, interpreting and reporting the results of studies. The ethical research principles in social sciences are truthfulness, thoroughness, objectivity and relevance. These, in a nutshell negate research misconducts of all fabrications, falsification and plagiarism.These do not, however, include honest errors and differences of opinion. Any significant departure from acceptable practice of research community is construed as research misconduct. (Mc Nabb, 2008). Ethical issues are broadly categorized into following categories:

Personal Ethical Pitfalls

1. Supervisor – Researcher's relationship issues,
2. Repetitive research problems,
3. Reliability, validity and objectivity of results,
4. Commercialization,
5. Inflated ego to learn innovative ideas.

Professional Ethical Pitfalls

1. Poor hypothesis, weak research methods and inappropriate statistical tools.
2. Declining professional ethical standards to maintain openness, integrity and transparency to avoid plagiarism.

3. Lack of training in research aptitude, commitment, creativity and responsiveness among students.
4. Lack of Interdisciplinary approach.
5. Poor quality of preparation, research design, appropriateness of research methodology and critically assessing research concepts and results.
6. Patronage among dons encouraging rivalry.
7. Plagiarism producing Xeroxed theses / Dissertations.
8. Ineffective mechanisms to monitor performance.

Socio-Political Ethical Pitfalls

1. Bureaucratic hurdles, manipulation and political consideration to influence research process.
2. No correlation between social research problems carried out and problems being faced by the society.
3. Research capacity of students to access digital and computational resources.
4. No encouragement from political leadership, bureaucracy, public opinion and media,
5. Lack of organic linkages between research quality and career advancement benefits.
6. Governmental apathy to recognize research output.
7. Compartmentalized knowledge generated in universities and research institutes.

These issues underline the deteriorating quality of the research in higher education. These issues revolve round the critical role of governance system of universities, bureaucracy, teaching departments, the supervisor and scholars.These have also pointed out that relationship between research supervisor and the candidates is not properly defined. There is no match between topic of research chosen by the candidates and expertise of the supervisor. The interaction between the candidates and the mentor is less frequent and mentor's role is restricted to providing guidelines and suggestions. Besides, political consideration, patronage, manipulation, sycophancy and mediocrity are vitiating the quality and objectivity (Ninam, 2007).

Integrity, honesty, hard work, behavioral control and faithfulness are the ethical parts of research. This is concerned about the possible mistreatment of human participants in research in order to pave a way for the correct perspectives in research. As a matter of fact, certain sort of ethical difficulties take place repeatedly in social relations research. There were instances of researchers, who have led their subjects to say or do things which violated their moral standards and about which they were later ashamed. Sometimes it happens to neglect the ethical part of the research, which is a great concern of the social fabric. There are several reasons why a researcher must be careful in the ethical area of the project. When a researcher conducts research on humans or organization where people are closely related, there must also be some regulation to protect human's subjectivity and privacy. Due to some unethical standards, scientific societies have formed codes of ethics for the treatment of participants. In the educational systems of social concerns, the research grants are legalized and researchers are expected to follow a set of rules provided by the government in order to ensure the ethical part of the project.

Research candidates have an obligation not only to protect the participants from the pitfalls in their research but also to provide knowledge needed in the area of research. The need for knowledge relevant to the promotion of human welfare and the solution of social problems is particularly acute. The research participant is, therefore, responsible for any misleading in the research and answerable to clarify the nature of the research including the reasons for the deception, to remove any harmful aftereffects of questionable practices used in research and to guarantee the subject's anonymity and the confidentiality of the data, including invasion on the privacy of research participant, withholding benefits from participants and failing to treat research participants fairly and to show them consideration and respect.

Some of the questionable practices which are grouped into are:

1. Involving people into research without their knowledge and concern.

2. Coercing people to participate.
3. Withholding from the participant the true nature of the research.
4. Deceiving the research participant.
5. Leading the research participants to commit acts which diminish their self-respect.
6. Violating the right to self-determination: research on behavior control and character change.
7. Exposing the research participant to physical or mental stress (Claira and Stuart, 2007).

1. Involving People into Research without Their Knowledge and Concern

Sometimes the researcher distorts the results in the research by assuming that the information would lead the participants to react in a negative way if data is recorded in the original form. If the information is put in the eyes of the public, it becomes an ethical issue of invasion of one's privacy. Therefore, the researcher, however has obligation to seek the permission of the participant and hence has infringed upon participant's right to make his or her own decision whether or not to participate.

The researcher must always seek ways to avoid the prospect of involuntary participation. If unsuccessful, the researcher must then carefully weigh the benefits of the research against its ethical costs. There are several types of studies in which this kind of problem is expected. In the field experiments, the participant's experiences are arranged in an order by the researcher.The less the researcher's procedure inconveniences the participants or involves them emotionally, the less severe the ethical question over engaging them in research without their knowledge or consent.

Apart from the fact that the studies of the type cited limit participant's rights to consent to activities in which they are to be involved, these experimental procedures concern social scientists because of the possibilities of their culminative impact on society. Some fear that as the research procedures become known through the mass media and through the textbooks many people will react to real crisis situation.

2. Coercing People to Participate

There are researchers who want people to participate in their research without participant's full knowledge. On the other hand, participants are forced to participate by various means and claim participant's consent. Ideally, consent should be obtained only after a potential subject has been given adequate information about the research in question. Sometimes potential participants are bribed or offered some incentives that they are unable to resist.This is the same case with people enticed by money, who are financially poor. With these means of attractions, a bridge is made between the researcher and the participants. It may be a case that the potential participants are not in sympathy with the research objectives and would not take part if allowed to decide for themselves. When potential participants are inexperienced and have unquestioned respect for the research candidates who approach them, have to create interpersonal trust. It does not follow, of course, that a modest description of the potential value of proposed research is out of order. To the contrary, it is one of the elements needed for an informed decision to participate.

3. Withholding from the Participant the True Nature of the Research

Another ethical part of the research is not to hide the true nature of research from the participant. Some participants may involve voluntarily in the research project because they were not told the true intent of the research. Participants may be frustrated or may react, when told in the latter part of the project. Some researchers reveal only part of the story, misleading the participants. Their function is to satisfy the participant's curiosity about what is transpiring.

When people consent to take part in the research without being told of its true characteristics, they are not giving what is commonly called their "informed" consent. Withholding information about research in which a person consents to participate is a questionable practice for reasons: the right of free choice has been curtailed and as a result, human dignity has been diminished. research candidates are obliged to avoid such acts if at all possible. If they cannot, they must give careful consideration to the ethical costs of carrying out the research and the values to be observed in doing so. Studies in which the true purpose is not revealed may attract consequences later.

4. Deceiving the Research Participant

Researcher may either withhold the information from the participants or provide part of the information to achieve the feedback. While some researchers hide the truth of the project, they may actively tell an untruth to the participants to pull out the information, which is not ethically right. Deliberate lying in the interest of participant's perceptions and actions goes directly against the ideology of integrity and honesty. Yet often the choice appears to be between carrying out such deception and deserting the research. Deception is planned for a number of reasons:

(a) To conceal the true purpose of the research.

(b) To conceal the true function of the participant's action.

(c) To conceal the participants experiences, when counter-questioned by a second party.

There are researchers who induce people with handsome attractions to achieve their purpose in the research project. Moral character is above the value of education itself. Therefore the ethical standard for the research in these areas are to be checked.

5. Misleading the Participants

There are several researchers who use procedures calculated to induce their own behavior to loose honesty, faithfulness and sincerity in their research. Some lead the participants to commit acts, which diminish their self-respect. To study the honesty, for example, the researcher creates an opportunity for the research participants to lie, cheat and steal.To study helping behavior one puts unsuspecting individuals in situations in which they may refuse to help when it is badly needed. To study resistance to authority, one pressures participants to obey orders they regard as wrong and harmful. Some researchers argue that the reactions of research participants who have been led to commit acts that threaten their self-respect should determine whether such practices should be continued.

Two shortcomings of such research of misleading are, one, researchers have no right to impose their educational services on others who have not requested them. The second is that the process of recognizing and changing one's personal weaknesses is complex and sensitive. To be constructive, it must take place in a supportive or a therapeutic context rather than in a brief and threatening laboratory confrontation. If we grant that practices threatening the research participant's self-respect are undesirable and yet appreciate the importance of the topic being studied with the aid of such practices. We may wish to ask whether degrees of undesirability may be distinguished among practices in common use.

6. Violating the Right to Self-determination

In some cases, researchers create situations that lead participants to commit acts such as cheating and harming others, which is a violation of one's right. It should be noted that this issue is independent of the nature of the behavior or character change produced in research. Temptations to be dishonest are to be judged ethically to see the effects on the society at large.

The origin of the questionable practice of violating the research participant's right to self-determination is the researcher's obligation to produce a science that is adequate for the task of guiding the development and modification of social behavior. Untruthful changes would not occur if the participants were given a free choice on the self-determination. They occur only because the investigators had discovered that influences that would lead them to change or as some would put it, the way to manipulate.

7. Exposing to Physical or Mental Stress

Human reactions to stress and behavior under stressful situations are considerable topics in the social relations. Stressful experiences are normally presented to research participants with fore warning, being mindful or unmindful. These stressful situations may sometimes attract negative reaction of the participants in individual or corporational way or may be complained upon legally. Even in the good attitude, a researcher has no right to expose the research participant to the physical or mental stress, which is an ethical concern of the social research.

Ethical Issues in Research Writing

As technical writing grows into a more common discipline, complicated questions concerning ethical standards seem to present themselves more frequently. Much of what is written by a writer will need to appeal to individuals of varying situational backgrounds and in this day of intense political correctness and moral responsibility, it is important to remember the ethical and other cultural issues associated with writing for diverse groups of people.

Perhaps the foremost ethical question that presents itself to technical writers revolves around the question "What makes a piece of writing acceptable to one's audience?" This question can be approached by remembering that the ultimate goal of any form of writing is to spark an interest in the reader that will cause her or him to follow the writer's thoughts to the end of the work. One way to ensure that the audience will remain attentive is to refrain from offending those who have expressed a desire to read those words. This issue is largely a matter of ethics and one that can harm or assist one's career in technical writing.

When beginning one's research for any project, four basic issues should be considered: audience, purpose, scope and prior knowledge. The writer should determine who his or her audience will be and for what purposes the audience will use the writer's knowledge. The audience's intended purposes will determine how broad or narrow to focus the scope of the information. Finally, the writer's prior knowledge of the given topic will determine how much time should be devoted to research, (Ann, Ann and Staples, 2001).

It is vital to take note that ethical issues are not limited to the field of education, but many questionable concerns can certainly present themselves in pedagogical situations. For example, when using a student (or a group of students) as a source of data for research, it is important to remain aware of his or her vulnerability, dignity and privacy. These three conditions come into question on a regular basis and are heavily debated by professionals in the field. The vulnerability of a human subject is of the greatest ethical importance. A researcher should always consider the mental and physical condition of the subject before translating his or her findings into a professionally written paper or article, as certain research conclusions could prove to be highly detrimental upon public release. The subject should be made aware of what she or he is foregoing by taking part in the research process, especially one that is planning to be released to the public. The ethical concern revolves around whether or not data gleaned from such research is beneficial enough to the end results of the project to warrant placing the subject in a compromising position by publishing his or her words or actions, regardless of given consent. (Anderson, 1998)

While some writers argue that it is acceptable to use any and all data obtained from research provided that pseudonyms are used when referring to their subjects in the body of their work or given that their findings are communicated in a respectful way, those concerned within the dignity of their subjects, as well as the dignity of the professional writing field and its future, disagree with these arguments, holding firm to their belief that the ethics involved are primary and without them, the final paper is undesirable (Cook, 2001).

Further, the privacy of one's subject should also play a vital role in the research process. Again, in pedagogical circumstances this becomes increasingly important, as many writers tend to argue the fact that he or she should be ethically permitted to use the personal writings and confidential conversations collected from his or her students as material for research.

In addition to the research process, ethical issues are increasingly important in the actual writing of the text. Many factors relating to modern interpretations of political correctness are making their presence known in the field of technical writing including the use of gender language, religious and/or cultural differences and sexual orientation. Issues of religious and cultural differences are key concerns for a researcher as the world continues to enlarge its global neighborhoods. It is often seen that a writer finds herself or himself writing for diverse audiences of many ethnicities and belief systems. It is important to write texts in such a way as to ensure an inoffensive tone when approaching a culturally diverse audience. (Claire & Stuart, 2000).

Another audience consideration that seems to especially affect technical writers, perhaps more than any other concept is that of educational differences. Keeping this in mind, an effective writer should consider the educational level of the audience. When the educational level of the audience is not known, it is wise to use straightforward speech that is capable of being understood by at least a majority of the audience or explain difficult words or concepts that may not be familiar to everyone listening to or reading what one has written. For example, words of medical terminology, engineering or computer terms and concepts used by various political entities should be clearly spelt out.

Plagiarism

At the intersection of language and culture lies a concept that we might call "langua-culture." In writing ones research paper, the researcher should document everything that he borrows – not only direct quotations and paraphrases but also information and ideas. Of course, common sense as well as ethics should determine what to document. A word related issue concerns copyright infringement. Because of the omnipresence of the Internet and the ease with which it is possible to download and duplicate Internet publications, many people think online materials are free to be reproduced and distributed at will.The truth is that most materials on the Internet, like most printed works, are protected by copyright law. Read carefully any special instructions or restrictions specified in the document or at the site.Whereas summaries, paraphrases, and brief quotations in research papers are normally permissible with appropriate acknowledgment, reproducing and distributing an entire copyrighted document or significant portions of it without obtaining permission from the author or publisher to do so is an infringement of copyright law and a legal offense, even if the violator acknowledges the source.

Derived from the Latin word plagiarius ("kidnapper"), plagiarism refers to a form of cheating that has been defined as "the false assumption of authorship: the wrongful act of taking the product of another person's mind, and presenting it as one's own" (Alexander Lindey, Plagiarism and Originality [New York: Harper, 1952]. To use another person's ideas or expressions in the writing without acknowledging the source is to plagiarize. Plagiarism, then, constitutes intellectual theft. Strictly speaking, it is a moral and ethical offense rather than a legal one, since most instances of plagiarism fall outside the scope of copyright infringement, a legal offense. Nonetheless, plagiarism often carries severe penalties, ranging from failure in a course to expulsion from school, (Gibaldi, 2000).

At all times during research and writing, guard against the possibility of inadvertent plagiarism by keeping careful notes that distinguish between one's own musings and thoughts and the material one gathers from others. Forms of plagiarism include the failure to give appropriate acknowledgment when repeating another's argument, or when presenting another's line of thinking. One may certainly use another persons' words and thoughts in his research paper, but the borrowed material must not seem as his own creation. It should be added as a reference by acknowledging.

Documenting Sources

Nearly all research builds on previous research. Researchers commonly begin a project by studying past work in the area and deriving relevant information and ideas from their predecessors. This process is largely responsible for the continual expansion of human knowledge. In presenting their work, researchers generously acknowledge their debts to predecessors by carefully documenting each source, so that earlier contributions receive appropriate credit. As one prepares a research he should similarly seek to build on the work of previous writers and researchers. And whenever he draws on another's work, he must also document his source by indicating what he borrowed – whether facts, opinions, or quotations – and where he borrowed it from.

MLA Style

In Modern Languages Association of America documentation style, as one acknowledges one's sources by keying brief parenthetical citations in the text to an alphabetical list of works that appears at the end of the paper. The parenthetical citation that concludes the following sentence is typical of MLA style.

Ancient writers attributed the invention of the monochord to Pythagoras, who lived in the sixth century BC (Marcuse 1975).

The citation "(Marcuse 1975)" tells readers that the information in the sentence was derived from page 197 of a work by an author named Marcuse. If readers want more information about this source, they can turn to the works-cited list, where, under the name Marcuse, they would find the following information, (Marcuse, Sibyl, A Survey of Musical Instruments, New York, Harper, 1975).

MLA style is not the only way to document sources. Many

disciplines have their own documentation systems. MLA style is widely used in the humanities. Although generally simpler and more economical than other documentation styles, it shares with most others its central feature: parenthetical citations keyed to a works-cited list. (Gibaldi, 2000)

Documentation styles differ according to discipline because they are shaped by the kind of research and scholarship undertaken. For example, in the sciences, where timeliness of research is crucial, the date of publication is usually given prominence. Thus, in the style recommended by the American psychological Association (APA), a typical citation includes the date of publication (as well as the abbreviation p. before the page number). Compare APA (Marcuse, a975, p.197) and MLA (Marcuse 197), parenthetical citations for the source.

In the humanities, where most important scholarship remains relevant for a substantial period, publication dates receive less attention: though always stated in the works-cited list, they are omitted in parenthetical references. An important reason for this omission is that many humanities scholars like to keep their texts as readable and as free of disruptions as possible. The entry is indented; second and subsequent lines are flush with the left margin (Marcuse, 1975).

In an entry in an APA style works-cited list, the date (in parenthesis) immediately follows the name of the author, (whose first name is written only as an initial), just the first word of the title is capitalized, and the publisher's full name is provided. In APA style, the first line of the entry is intended; second and subsequent lines are flush with the left margin, (Gibaldi, 2000) APA Marcuse, S. (1975), A Survey of Musical Instruments, New York, Harper and Row.

By contrast, in an MLA-style entry, the author's name appears as given in the work (normally in full), every important word of the title is capitalized, the publisher's name is shortened, and the publication date is placed at the end. In MLA style, the first line of the entry is flush with the left margin, and second and subsequent lines are indented. This formal helps readers locate author's names in the alphabetical listing (Marcuse, Sibyl, A Survey of Musical Instruments, Harper, 1975).

There are two issues related to plagiarism that do not deal with outside sources.

1. A candidate submitting a course, the paper he prepared for the previous course. This practice is said to be a kind of self-plagiarism. If he wants to rework on the paper he has to get prior permission from his research supervisor. In collaborative research, joint participation in research and writing credit should be given to all contributors (Gibaldi, 2000).

Copying others' work and turning it into one's own is not new, and the openness of the Internet has made retrieval of solutions and answers a breeze for students (Suarez & Martin, 2001). The problem of Plagiarism could possibly plague blog entries. However, Oravec, (2003) argued that the availability of blogs to the wider internet audience could well work against the problem. Students will be able to view each others' work in the individual blogs and each student can act as an extra pair of eyes to prevent one another from conveniently copying others work. Peer pressure may help to reduce the likelihood of plagiarism, as one would not want to copy and be faulted by this peers, (University News, 47(50) December 14-20, 2009).

7

PARTICIPATORY EVALUATION

Introduction

Any given social reality is never static, fixed or dead. Its life and movement are the result of a long time struggle, tension and conflict. As such, reality is not just a given fact or a furnished product which will remain static so that it can be easily assessed and evaluated. Hence, evaluation does not concern itself with what is, as much as with what can be. It dwells on alternatives to an oppressive reality. It stands as an important and useful tool for unmasking and criticizing any situation that negates human being, his dignity and worth. While evaluation literally means placing a value on results attained, it is the systematic determination of merit, worth and significance of something or someone.

Evaluation is often used to characterize and apprise subjects of interest in a wide range of human enterprises including the arts, business, computer science, criminal justice, education, engineering, foundations and non-profit organizations, religion, government, healthcare and other human services.

It is to analyze and understand what has happened and how various elements have caused certain events or situations to come about. It helps to integrate and consolidate learning, to bridge from the smaller to a larger scope, to reflect and summarize and to tie together loose ends. Above all, it helps the people involved in the program to measure the results achieved against the goals they have set for themselves and to identify the strengths and impacts or the weaknesses and drawbacks of the program and thus make concrete efforts to rectify them.

(http:llen.wikipedia.org/wiki/evaluation)

Evaluation or criticism should be positive as well as negative. It is usually easier to be negative about a research report, to say what strikes one as wrong with it, than to be positive about the report, to make clear what its good aspects are. But it is important to explain what one finds good in a research report as well as what one finds bad. One should look for and comment on, the good things as well as the bad.

In examining a report of research project, or thesis with a view towards evaluating how well the research is done, one needs to consider at least the following questions:

- Is there a well defined and understandable purpose? In the report, the purpose should be stated explicitly ideally, it should be expressed in the form of a testable hypothesis.
- Are the data that were used truly pertinent to the purpose? Are they the best data that could have been used for the purpose?
- Are the data gathered properly? For example, if sampling is involved, are the data obtained by an adequately random method?
- Were the data meant to be suitably studied and analyzed?
- Are the reported results based strictly on the outcome of the study or analysis of the data? Or are there findings that seem unsupported by the analysis?
- Does the investigator's interpretation of the results make sense? Does the interpretation appear to reflect in a reasonable way both the results and the overall situation or problem? One needs to think hard and carefully about the foregoing questions in evaluating the research report.

(http://www.gslis.utexas.edu/nwy//ys/evaluation gres.html.). IRLIS Material, (Retrieved on 12.09.06).

Evaluation of Methods and Techniques

Evaluation methodologically is diverse, using both qualitative methods and quantitative methods; it includes case studies, survey research, statistical analysis and model building among others. A more detailed list of methods, techniques and approaches for conducting evaluations would include the following:

. Action research
. Interview
. Marketing research
. Course evaluation
. Observational techniques
. Data mining
. Discourse analysis
. Statistical process control
. Environment scanning
. Appreciative inquiry
. Participant observation
. Assessment
. Case Study
. Policy analysis
. Strategic planning
. Factor analysis
. Structure interviewing
. Feasibility study
. Systems theory
. Field Experiment
. Total Quality Management
. Inquiry
. Triangulation
. Cost-benefit analysis
. Quantitative research
. Advanced Product Quality Planning
. Questionnaire
. Sampling
. Self assessment
. Opinion polling
. Alternative assessment
. Organizational learning
. Ethnography
. Statistical survey
. Experiment
. Experimental techniques
. Statistics
. Change management
. Process improvement
. Consensus decision-making
. Project management.
. Content analysis
. Qualitative research
. Conversation analysis
. Quality management

(http://en.wikipedia.org/wiki/evaluation (Retrieved on 12.09.06)

Participatory Evaluation of Data

A clear insight on participatory evaluation will be of great help in any study about its pros and cons. A few illustrations from the range of ways participatory evaluation can be understood. Greenwood and

Levin (1998) viewed that, "Participatory evaluation aims to create a learning process for the program recipients that will help them in their effort to reach desired goals."

Jackson (1998) suggests that, "Participatory evaluation is a process of self-assessment, collective knowledge production and cooperative action in which the stakeholders in a development intervention participate substantively in the identification of the evaluation issues, the design of the evaluation, the collection and analysis of the data and the action taken as a result of the evaluation findings."

Further, Patton (1990) says, "One of the negative connotations often associated with evaluation is that it is something done to people. Participatory evaluation, in contrast, is a process controlled by the people in the program of community. It is something they undertake as a formal, reflective process for their own development and empowerment."

Thus, a participatory evaluation can be safely addressed as a method of assessing a development program. Its purpose is to encourage the autonomous organization and creativity of the group since the objective of this evaluation is the people and their development of knowledge for the sake of control and study.

Participatory evaluation program needs to develop within a commonly accepted frame of reference: making it a joint endeavor with equal participation of the people in designing the program, in adapting it better to their needs.

Classification of Approaches

The given table 7.1 is used to summarize each approach in terms of four attributes – organizer, purpose, strengths and weaknesses. The organizer represents the main considerations or clues practitioners use to organize a study.

The purpose represents the desired outcome for a study at a very general level. Strengths and weaknesses represent other attributes that should be considered, when deciding whether to use the approach for a particular study. The following narrative highlights differences between approaches grouped together.

Table 7.1

Summery of Approaches for Conducting Evaluations

Approaches	*Attribute Organizer*	*Purpose*	*Key Strengths*	*Key* Weaknesses
Politically controlled	Threats, fame.	Get, keep or increase, influence power or money.	Secure evidence, advantageous to the client in a conflict.	Violates the principle of full frank disclosure.
Public relations	Propaganda needs.	Create positive public image.	Secure evidence most likely to bolster public support.	Violates the principles of balanced reporting, justified conclusions and objectives
Experimen- -tal research	Causal relationships.	Determine causal relationships between variables.	Strongest paradigm for determining causal relationships.	Requires controlled setting, limits range of evidence, focuses primarily on results.
Management information systems	Scientific efficiency.	Continuou- -sly supply evidence needed to fund, direct control programs.	Gives managers detailed evidence about complex programs.	Human service variables are rarely amenable to the narrow, quantitative definitions needed.
Testing programs	Individual differences.	Compare test scores ofindividuals	Produces valid reliable.	Data usually only on testee performance.

		groups to selected norms.	evidence in many performance areas.	overemphasi--zes test-taking skills, can be poor sample of what is taught or expected.
Objectives -based	Objectives.	Relates outcome to objectives.	Commonsense appeal, widely used, uses behavioral objectives testing technologies.	Leads to terminal evidence often too narrow to provide basis for judging to value a program.
Content analysis	Content of an communica--tion.	Describe & draw con--clusions about a communi--cation.	Allows for unobtrusive analysis of large volumes of unstruc--tured, symbolic materials.	Sample may be unrepre--sentative yet overwhel--ming in volume analysis design often overly simplistic for question.
Decision-oriented	Decision.	Provide a knowledge value base for making defending decisions.	Encourages use of evalua--tion to plan implement needed programs. Helps justify decision about plans actions.	Necessary collaboration between evaluator decision-maker provides opportunity to bias results.

Policy studies	Broad issues.	Identify and assess potential costs benefits of competing policies.	Provide general direction for broadly focused actions.	Often corrupted or subverted by politically motivated actions of participants.
Consumer - oriented	Generalized needs values, effects.	Judge the relative merits of alternative goods services.	Independent appraisal to protect practitioners consumers from bad products services. High public credibility.	Might not help practi- -tioners do a better job. Requires credible competent evaluators.
Accredita- -tion / certification	Standards guidelines.	Determine if institutions, programs personal should be approved to perform specified functions.	Helps public make informed decisions about quality of organi- -zations qualifications of personnel.	Standards guidelines typically emphasize intrinsic criteria to the exclusion of outcome measures.
Adversary	"Hot" issues.	Present the pros & cons of an issue.	Ensures balanced presentations of represented issue perspectives	Can discourage cooperation, heighten animosities.
Client-centered	Specific concerns issues.	Foster understan- -ding of activities how they are valued in a given setting from a variety of perspectives.	Practitioners are helped to conduct their own evaluation.	Low external credibility, susceptible to bias in favor of participants.

Source: **(Stufflebeam & Webster, 1980)**

Criteria for Valuation of Resources

- Authorship and Affiliation
- Accuracy / Verifiability
- Objectivity
- Audience
- Currency
- Content / Purpose
- Comparison to Other Similar Resources

Asking the following questions about the criteria listed above will help to decide if the sources are authoritative and useful. And, of course, these questions apply to print library sources, as well as World Wide Web resources.

Authorship and Affiliation

- Who is the author of the book / article / Web site?
- Is the author a well-known and well-regarded authority?
- Mainly print resources: How reputable is the publisher?
- Has the author listed her/his credentials (e.g., education, occupation, etc.) for being an authority on the material?
- Does the author's email address appear so that one can contact her/him for further information?
- Does the author note her/his institutional affiliation (university, government, organization, etc.)?

Accuracy / Verifiability

Nothing could be further from the truth. So, it is critical to judge the veracity of the information presented even more vigilantly than in print resources.

- How reliable and free from error (typographically, factually and conceptually) is the information?

- Are the researcher's methods for obtaining data or conducting research clearly stated so that the study may be duplicated?
- Does the researcher demonstrate knowledge of scientific theories and techniques?
- Mainly for print resources: Does the material include a bibliography?

Objectives

- Is the material presented as fact or opinion?
- Is the information presented with a minimum of bias?
- To what extent is the information trying to sway the opinion of the audience?

Audience

- Is the material sufficiently scholarly, yet not so complicated that one can't understand it?

Currency

- When is the material published?
- For Web resources: Is the update prominently noted?
- Does the material present the latest thinking on the topic?
- Is currency an important factor for the material that is presented?

Content/Purpose

- Is the purpose (to inform, explain, persuade or entertain) of the material apparent?
- What topics are included in the material?
- Are the topics that are included explored in appropriate depth?
- If the material is available in both print and Web format, the does coverage differ between versions?
- Is supporting material, such as bibliographies, indexes, charts, maps and other graphics, included and correctly attributed?
- How comprehensive is the coverage of the material?

Comparison to Other Similar Materials

- Are there other resources that present the same information and how do they compare, generally to the medinial?
- Given the answers to the above questions, is the material authoritative and suitable for research?

Different Ways of Evaluating Materials

As one does the research each step is very important. From the time the researcher starts to gather material / data, defines each term, makes hypothesis, states research problem, and evaluates the materials, all the steps are of equal importance because all of these rely on each other. The shape and the value of what is produced as a research report will be significantly determined by how well the researcher does this analysis and evaluation. When the research has been completed, the original terms of reference should be reviewed to see how far the results of research have met the original needs the terms of reference expressed. In the case of research which is essentially a program evaluation, it may also be important to see who needs to take action on the research. This may also apply to feasibility studies.

Evaluating Materials / Data Analysis / Content Analysis

Evaluating Materials

When the research has been completed, the original terms of reference should be reviewed to see how far the results of the research have met the original needs, the terms of reference expressed. After the data are gathered they must be tabulated and statistically analyzed to determine the correlation between variables and what their significance is. How can a researcher go about evaluating the materials which he / she have gathered for a research project? There are different methods of evaluating materials.

Critical Method

Critical method is based upon two presuppositions –

1. The first presupposition is that research materials can be

properly understood only when viewed in reference to their original cultural – historical context. The language is also an important factor as the meaning of the old words change with time, new words evolve, and even the same word in the same time period can have different meaning among different groups of people. No area of research is free of socio – cultural influences of people.

2. Second presupposition is that materials gathered during the research are not necessarily free from error and it can be misleading and misinterpreting. Sometimes what happens is that some people regard some findings as 'facts' which may actually be biased perceptions of reality which rationalize self–interest. Materials gathered during research will often be not only diverse but at times even contradictory. Therefore, due to these reasons, researchers must examine and evaluate the materials. (Abreo, 2000)

Procedures in Analysis and Evaluation

Procedures described in this assignment are based on the tools provided by Mabry (1999). They are authentication, types of source, credentials of the writer, reliability of the material, representativeness of the data and corroboration. Authentication under this one should check is that a particular material comes from original source. Is the data genuine? Has it been misidentified? Is it only a forgery? In order to establish the same, the researcher need to see the following factors: Authorship for modern publishing material, the determination of authorship may not be the problem e.g., authorship is the main problem in the critical study of a portion of the Bible. Where there is no external way of checking authorship it may be necessary to rely upon internal evidence such as main idea.

Date

When is the material written? Where the date is unknown, various tests can be employed. Look at other editions, translations of the same author, style of the language, and the relationship of the knowledge with the author etc. By examining the above issues one can establish the correct date. Textual Accuracy: is the text accurate in substance and composition? Does it contain errors? Errors in transmission may be of direct kind.

Sources

The second tool in evaluation is the values of materials, which are collected in research. Is the material coming from origina sources? After research materials have been gathered the researcher needs to make distinction between primary and secondary data. The value of data will also depend upon whether they have direct or circumstantial evidence.

Direct evidence consists of eyewitness reports and other material by persons who were present at an event being studied. For example, circumstantial evidence consists of material from which inferences can be drawn about what happened at an event but which one directly witness to that event. The research is concerned with finding a persuasive answer to a question or problem. Primary materials will be more valuable than secondary materials.

Credentials of the Writer

The value of the secondary material can be estimated by the following qualifications:

What else has this author written?

How do others regard him in the same discipline?

What sources did the writer use?

Who is the publisher? Is the publisher reliable?

Is the writer qualified in the area in which he or she is writing?

This does not mean that a researcher should automatically reject material outside of the area of an author's original training or the area for which an author is best known.

Reliability of the material: In what ways one can assure that the materials, researchers have are reliable? To what extent is a writer biased, which prejudices his or her work?

Representativeness of the Data

Researcher has to recognize that even when one has collected all available written material, the data is still not necessarily representative. How much was the researcher involved in the matter? Whether it was from the published materials or he/she himself/ herself went to the concerned place for collecting and investigating the data.

Corroboration

Corroboration means examining the researcher's materials to see how far data from different sources are in agreement. Relying upon data from single source or from only a few sources can be very risky because other sources might provide contradictory evidence. If primary material from several writers witness to the same event then a high value can be assigned to that material. This is one of the reasons why in the Christian traditions a high value has been given to the synoptic gospels. They provide similar accounts, which, despite certain differences, are in much agreement about the life and ministry of Jesus. The evaluation of data is a crucial step in the research process. If data separates the 'valuable' from the 'not so valuable' it brings good research.

Validitation

"Validitation means cross-checking information from different sources to ensure consistency, and agreements between sources." Analysis is a part of validitation, and both sides of an argument, or contrasting perceptions, should be included in the final analysis or report, (Kothari, 1999).

Evaluating Source Materials

Source material forms the basis of written work. Therefore all of it should be reliable, accurate and authoritative.

Trustworthiness of Source

Trustworthiness of sources collected is very important. How can one know whether the material collected is trustworthy or not? It can be divided it into three ways-

1. The Most Trustworthy Sources:-

The primary research reports in referred journals, referred books.

e.g., – MLA handbook for writers of research papers.

Reviews in referred journals

e.g., Science bulletin.

2. Moderate Trustworthy sources:-

Text Books

Articles in popular science journals, referred books.

e.g., Psychology Today, University news, TBT journal

Articles in magazines and newspapers

e.g., India today, Times of India.

3. The Least Trustworthy Sources:-

The Internet

Television or Radio

How to Determine Trustworthy Sources?

To determine the trustworthiness one needs to check whether the material is relevant to assignment topic, its currency, reliability and accuracy.

- Is the information relevant?
- Is the format or medium of the information useful for the assignment or not?
- Is the information of primary or secondary source?
- Is the information sufficient?
- Whom does it direct to – general or specialized audience?

To Determine Currency

- When was the information published / created / compiled or produced?
- Is the information regularly updated and how often?
- Is the information still valid for the topic?

To Determine the Reliability

- Who is the author/producer/?
- Does the information come from authoritative source?

To Determine Accuracy

- How is the information presented? If it is factual it should be well documented so that its accuracy can be verified.
- Is the information biased? Check the language to see if it is objective and impartial or emotionally charged.

Evaluating Scientific Sources

While evaluating the scientific sources it's important to adopt more specific criteria, especially the journal articles that are reporting empirical research. The scientific merits of the source material should be evaluated in particular and for the soundness of the methodology that was used in the scientific research the following should be checked for:

1. Does the materials collected rely on the empirical evidences.
2. Is it utilizing the relevant concepts?
3. What predictions can be made? Is it resulting into probabilistic predictions?
4. Is the methodology known to all concerned for critical scrutiny and testing the conclusions through replication? .
5. Does it aim at formulating most general axioms?

The scientific method encourages a rigorous, impersonal mode of procedure dictated by the demands of logic and objective procedures (Mary, 2004).

Analysis

After the data have been collected, the researcher moves to the task of analyzing them. The analysis of data requires a number of closely related operations such as establishments of categories, the application of these categories to raw data through coding, tabulation and then drawing statistical interferences. It is an objective research technique for inferring the characteristics and cause and effect of communication. It is an unobtrusive research. According to Young (1975) 'content analysis is a research technique for systematic and objective and quantitative description of content of research procured through interviews, questionnaires, schedules and other linguistic expressions, written or oral. It is concerned with the ideas contained in it'.

Criteria for Evaluation of a Research Report, Article and Thesis

I. Aims

(a) Precise identification of problem area, often including

specification of independent and dependent variables and identification of target population.

(b) Sufficient clarity and conciseness for indexing of title.

(c) Effective arrangement of words in title. (William 1967)

II. The Problem

(A) Description and statement of problem

1. Statement of basic (felt) difficulty or problem situation – significance and importance of the problem area in either basic or applied research.
2. Careful analysis of known and suspected facts and explanation of existing information and knowledge that may have some bearing on problem-the spelling out of specific factors giving rise to the basic difficulty, or their interrelationships and of their relevance to the problem area.
3. Soundness of the logic underlying selection of variables or factors to be studied and expression of their relationship to the problem area.
4. Systematic and orderly presentation of the interrelationships of relevant facts and concepts underlying the problem.
5. Clear identification of the problem statement through use of an appropriate heading or paragraph caption (the same requirement holding for other major categories of the research).
6. Succinct, precise and unambiguous statement of the research problem (including the delineation of independent, dependent and classificatory variables), of the major questions to be resolved, or of the objectives to be investigated.
7. Distinction (if required) between problems of questions that are either factually oriented or value oriented.
8. Distinction in the instance of theoretically oriented research or of basic research between the purpose, which is often goal-oriented or instrumental in relation to certain pragmatic objectives and the research problem which is primarily the noting of changes (possible cause and effect

relationships) relative to operationally formulated research hypotheses.

(B) Sufficient delimitation of the problem area-narrowing of the scope without becoming concerned with a trivial problem.

(C) Review and evaluation of the literature pertinent to problem areas.

1. Adequacy and relevance of the previous investigation cited with reference to the basic difficulty posed, design of the current investigation, procedures followed, and projected analysis of data.
2. Appropriate development of a rationale or theoretical framework from the research studies cited with reference to the current problem under investigation.

(D) Clear-cut statement of the conceptions, assumptions or postulates underlying the problem being investigated.

(E) Precise statement of (1) hypotheses or (2) deduced consequences of theories or (3) the objectives of a study (objectives being most common in survey and descriptive research).

1. Hypotheses involving relationships and comparisons.
2. Presentation of deducible consequences or predictions (if any) that are logically consistent with a hypothesis (i.e., antecedent-consequent statement: If A exists, then B follows).

(F) Definition of terms

1. Clarity in the definitions of key terms and variables (especially constructs).
2. Use of operational definitions whenever possible.

III. Design and Methodology (Procedures)

(A) Logic, Structure and Strategy of Study carefully delineated.

1. Distinction made between whether the research involves variables manipulated and controlled by the investigator (usually found in experimental research) or whether an ex post facto situation exists involving the analysis of data already

available or collected as in most field studies and correlational investigations.

2. Appropriate use of paradigms, flow charts or schematic models.
3. Information concerning the possible operation of selective drop-out and survival of the fittest.

(B) Clear Description of Samples Studied.

1. Mode of selection of subject cited (e.g., random assignment, matching, voluntary participation or convenience by being available).
2. Data regarding how representative a sample is relative to a population.
3. Information concerning the possible operation of selective drop-out and survival of the fittest.

(C) Adequate information pertaining to the reliability, validity and standardization properties of instrumentation: psychometric characteristic of scales or tests used.

(D) Sufficient description of operational or field procedures followed in the collection of data-where, when and how data were obtained.

(E) Coordination of specification of the relationship between the null (statistical) hypotheses and the research (problem) hypotheses.

(F) Appropriateness of the statistical treatment and data processing procedures.

(G) Evidence of a preparatory pilot study having been conducted.

(H) Procedure clearly enough described so that other investigators can replicate (repeat) the study performed under essentially comparable conditions in the future.

(I) Statement of methodological assumption such as adequacy of reliability and validity of measures, responsibility and validity of measures, representativeness of samples, fulfillment of appropriate requirements for carrying out statistical tests.

IV. Presentation and Analysis of Data

(A) Logical and orderly exposition in terms of the framework of the hypotheses, deductions, objectives or questions asked in conjunction with the statement of the problem.

1. Objective rather than subjective or speculative presentation.
2. Analysis consistent with and supported by the facts obtained.
3. Absence of overgeneralizations or sweeping statements that go beyond the data.
4. Relationships of the findings of previously cited research explicitly shown.
5. Negative findings relative to the hypotheses as well as positive findings presented with minimal distortion or bias.
6. Uncontrolled factors influencing data outcomes appropriately cited and discussed.
7. Weaknesses in the data honestly conceded and discussed with appropriate emphasis.
8. Lack of confusion between facts and inferences clearly shown-separation of analysis of findings from interpretation and discussion of findings.
9. Resolution of contradictions, inconsistencies or misleading elements in the findings.

(B) Appropriate and clear use of charts, tables, figures and graphs.

V. Summary and Conclusion

(A) Precise and accurate statement of (1) the problem, (2) the methodology followed and (3) the findings without the introduction of new or irrelevant information.

(B) Conclusions at a scope and level of generality justified by the data presented.

(C) Appropriate caution exercised and necessary qualifications made in drawing conclusions.

(D) Conclusions in a form that other investigators can understand and subsequently verify.

(E) Conclusions coordinated with the tentative acceptance or rejection of the research hypotheses presented or with the objectives or questions posed.

(F) New questions set forth for possible investigation-recommendations for additional research in the problem area study.

(G) Recommendations concerning implementation of the research findings when appropriate relative to the objectives stated in the purpose of the investigation most frequently encountered in survey studies and action research (William, 1967).

Table - 7.2

Form for the Evaluation of an Article

Characteristic	1 Completely Independent	2 Poor	3 Mediocre	4 Good	5 Excellent
1. Problem is clearly stated					
2. Hypotheses are clearly stated					
3. Problem is significant					
4. Assumptions are clearly stated					
5. Limitations of the study are stated					
6. Important terms are defined					
7. Relationship of problem to previous research is made clear					
8. Research design is described fully					
9. Research design is					

appropriate for the solution of the problem	
10. Research design is free of specific weaknesses	
11. Population and sample are described	
12. Method of sampling is appropriate	
13. Data-gathering methods or procedures are described	
14. Data-gathering methods or procedures are appropriate to the solution of the problem	
15. Data-gathering methods or procedures are utilized correctly	
16. Validity and reliability of the evidence gathered are established	
17. Appropriate methods are selected to analyze the data	
18. Methods utilized in analyzing the data are applied correctly	
19. Results of the analysis are presented clearly	
20. Conclusions are clearly stated	
21. Conclusions are substantiated by the	

evidence presented	
22. Generalizations are confined to the population from which the sample was drawn	
23. Report is clearly written	
24. Report is logically organized	
25. Tone of the report displays an unbiased, impartial scientific Attitude	

8

PROCESSING AND ANALYSIS OF DATA

Processing

Analysis of data needs good planning. Appropriate, statistical techniques and their application are necessary to have a scientific approach to research. The data, after collection, has to be processed and analyzed in accordance with the outline laid down for the purpose at the time of developing the research plan. This is essential for a scientific study and for ensuring that we have all relevant data for making contemplated comparisons and analysis.

Technically speaking, processing implies editing, coding, classification and tabulation of collected data so that they are amenable to analysis. The term analysis refers to the computation of certain measures along with searching for patterns of relationship that exist among data-groups. Thus, "in the process of analysis, relationships or differences supporting or conflicting with original or new hypotheses should be subjected to statistical tests of significance to determine with what validity data can be said to indicate any conclusions, (Giles, 1974).

Processing Operations

Editing

Editing of data is a process of examining the collected raw data. Editing is done to assure that the data are accurate, consistent with other facts gathered, uniformly entered, as complete as possible and have been well arranged to facilitate coding and tabulation. Two stages at which editing should be done, one can talk of field editing and central editing. Field editing consists in the review of the reporting forms by the investigator for completing (translating or rewriting) what the latter has written in abbreviated and or in illegible form at the time of recording the respondents' responses. This type of editing is necessary in view of the fact that individual writing styles often can be difficult for others to decipher. This sort of editing should be done as soon as possible after the interview.

Central editing should take place when all forms or schedules have been completed and returned. This type of editing implies that all forms should get a thorough editing by a single editor in a small study and by a team of editors in case of a large inquiry. Editor(s) may correct the obvious errors such as entry in the wrong place. In case of inappropriate or missing replies, the editor can sometimes determine the proper answer by reviewing the other information in the schedule. At times, the respondent can be contacted for clarification. The editor must strike out the answer if the same is inappropriate and he has no basis for determining the correct answer or the response. In such a case an editing entry of 'no answer' is called for. All the wrong replies, which are quite obvious, must be dropped from the final results, especially in the context of mail surveys.

Editors must keep in view several points while performing their work: (a) they should be familiar with instructions given to the interviewers and coders as well as with the editing instructions supplied to them for the purpose. (b) While rejecting original entry for one reason or another, they should just draw a single line on it so that the same may remain legible. (c) They must make entries (if any) on the form in some distinctive color and that too in a standardized form. (d) They should initial all answers which they change or supply. (e) Editor's initials and the date of editing should be placed on each completed form or schedule (Emory, 1976).

Editing is the first step in data processing. Editing is the process of examining the data collected in questionnaires / schedules to detect errors and omission and to see that they are corrected and the schedules prepared for tabulation. When the whole data collection is over a final and thorough check up is made. Mildred B. Parten (1959) points out that the editor is responsible for seeing that the data are (1) as accurate as possible (2) consistent with other facts secured, (3) uniformly entered, (4) as complete as possible, (5) acceptable for tabulation and (6) arranged to facilitate coding and tabulation.

Editing is also undertaken to determine whether or not a specific interview is acceptable in the light of objectives of the project. Editing for Tabulation and preparation of the data forms for tabulation must include an operational procedure for accepting, modifying or rejecting individual questionnaires. Incorrect answers should be discarded. Inconsistent answers must also be discarded. When the reply indicates a modified or qualified response to another question, the change should be indicated. Numerical answers must be converted to similar units. Where numerical answers are to be tabulated in classes, the editors should indicate the proper classification on the data form. Answers should be allocated to the proper category of response. The investigator should indicate which of the replies are worth verbatim reproduction.

Coding

Coding refers to the process of assigning numerals or other symbols to answers so that responses can be put into a limited number of categories or classes. Such classes should be appropriate to the research problem under consideration. Every class is defined in terms of only one concept. Coding is necessary for efficient analysis and through it several replies may be reduced to a small number of classes which contain the critical information required for analysis. Coding decisions should usually be taken at the designing stage of the questionnaire. This makes it possible to pre-code the questionnaire choices and which in turn is helpful for computer tabulation as one can straightly key punch from the original questionnaires. But in case of hand coding some standard method may be used. One such standard method is to code in the margin with a colored pencil. The other method can be to transcribe the data from the questionnaire to a coding sheet. Whatever method is adopted, one should see that coding errors are altogether eliminated or reduced to the minimum level.

Rules for Coding

1. Give code numbers for each respondent for identification: Generally while giving identification number, different digits are used to identify the area, institution and the department also.
2. Give code numbers for each question.

3. Give code numbers for each response. In this context categorization assumes significance.
4. Give numbers for qualitative responses also.
5. Do not delegate the work of categorization to others. Researcher himself should undertake the work, because categorization is not a routine work.
6. Prepare the coding frame.
7. Decide on the instructions to coders.
8. Prepare and supply coders' instruction manual.
9. May take the services of trained coders with close supervision.
10. Carefully scrutinize every coded item in the initial stages of coding.
11. Afterwards have a random checking of the coded times.
12. The researcher himself should decide on any change in coding due to change in the nature of data or importance of data after collection (Saravanavel, 2009).

Classification

Most research studies result in a large volume of raw data which must be reduced into homogeneous groups if one has to get meaningful relationships. This fact necessitates classification of data which happens to be the process of arranging data in groups or classes on the basis of common characteristics. Data having a common characteristic are placed in one class and in this the entire data gets divided into a number of groups or classes. Classification can be one of the following two types, depending upon the nature of the phenomenon involved.

1. Classification according to Attributes: As stated above, data are classified on the basis of common characteristics which can either be descriptive (such as literacy, sex, honesty, etc.,) or numerical (such as weight, height, income etc.). Descriptive characteristics refer to qualitative phenomenon which cannot be measured quantitatively; only their presence or absence in an individual item can be noticed. Data obtained this way on the basis of certain attributes are known as statistics of attributes and their classification is said to be classification according to attributes.

2. Classification according to Class-intervals: Unlike descriptive characteristics, the numerical characteristics refer to quantitative phenomenon which can be measured through some statistical units. Data relating to income, production, age, weight, etc. come under this category. Such data are known as statistics of variables and are classified on the basis of class intervals.

Classification or categorization is the process of grouping the statistical data under various understandable homogenous groups for the purpose of convenient interpretation. A uniformity of attributes is the basic criterion for classification; and the grouping of data is made according to similarity. Classification becomes necessary where there is diversity in the data collected for meaningful presentation and analysis. A good classification should have the characteristics of clarity, homogeneity, equality of scale, purposefulness and accuracy.

Objectives of Classification: The objectives of the classification are given below:

1. Through classification, the complex scattered and haphazard data is organized into concise, logical and intelligible form.
2. Through Classification, it is possible to make the characteristics of similarities and dis-similarities clear.
3. Through classification, comparative study is possible.
4. Through classification, understanding of the significance is made easier and thereby good deal of human energy is saved.
5. Underlying unity amongst different items is made clearly expressed.
6. Data is so arranged that analysis and generalization becomes possible.

Types of Classification: Classification is of two types, viz., quantitative classification, which is on the basis of variables or quantity; and qualitative classification (classification according to attributes). The former is the way of grouping the variables, say, quantifying the variables in cohesive groups, while the latter groups the data on the basis of attributes or qualities. Again, it may be multiple classification or dichotomous classification. The former is the way of making many (more than two) groups on the basis of some quality or attributes, while the latter is the classification into two groups on the basis of the presence or absence of a certain quality, (Michael, 1985).

Classification is made on periodical basis: In this type of classification the data belonging to a particular time or period is put under one class. Classification on Geographical basis: In this type of classification, the data has been collected from different places and placed in different classes. The researcher must properly classify his data into the required categories. The principle for classification has to be based on the problem under study or the hypothesis. For example, if the problem is the "extent of poverty", income, consumption, saving etc., may be the required categories.

Content Analysis

Content analysis is an objective research technique for inferring the characteristics, causes and effects of communication. It is an unobtrusive research. According to Pauline (1975), 'Content Analysis' is a research technique for systematic, objective and quantitative description of content of research produced through interviews, questionnaires, schedules and other linguistic expressions, written or oral. It means categorization or classification of data in to different categories or groups. It is a method of studying 'communications' developed in U.S.A. as "Communication Research". Content analysis is concerned less with the style of the text than the ideas contained in it. Thus it can be considered as the application of the canon of scientific research to analyze communication content. Content analysis cannot be applied to all documents. Content analysis is usually applicable to sociological analysis and not to the historical criticism. It requires the researcher to use his judgment in making decisions about data.

Objectives

The objective of Content Analysis is to convert recorded 'raw' phenomena into data which can be treated essentially in a scientific manner so that a body of knowledge may be built up. More specifically, content analysis must be conducted so as (1) to create reproducible or objective data, (2) which are susceptible to measurement and quantitative treatment, (3) have significance for some systematic theory and (4) may be generalized beyond the specific set of materials analyzed. Through content analysis, it is possible to make a comparative study of various levels of communications. It helps in construction and application of communication standards.

Content Analysis is a method of social research that aims at the analysis of the content – qualitative and / quantitative of documents, books, newspapers, magazines and other forms of written material. According to Berelson (1952), "content analysis is a research technique for the objective, systematic and quantitative description of the manifested content of communication". The word 'communication' here refers to "available written material or print media". The word 'manifest' means "which is presented outwardly". It thus excludes the 'implied meaning'. According to Eckhardt and Ermann (1977), as a qualitative technique, content analysis is directed towards more subjective information such as attitudes, motives and values, while a quantitative method is employed when determining the time frequency or duration of the event. In the latter context, it also makes inferences about conduct, intentions, ideologies, sentiments and values of individuals and groups.

The content (in content analysis) may be manifest or latent. The former refers to the visible actual parts of the text as manifested in the document, i.e., sentences, paragraphs and so on. It involves counting frequencies of appearance of the research unit. The latter is the underlying or implied meaning conveyed. Here, the researcher reads between the lines and analyses the hidden meaning significant for the object of the study. Gardner (1975) describes it as "a research method for investigating problems in which the content of communication serves as a basis of inference". At another stage, he (ibid) says: "Content analysis is a technique for making inferences by systematically and objectively identifying specified characteristics of messages (communications)."

Characteristics of Content Analysis

Gardner (1975) has referred to four characteristics of content analysis as under:

1. **Objectivity**, i.e., carrying out analysis on the basis of explicitly formulated rules which will enable two or more persons to obtain the same results from the same documents.

2. **Systematic,** i.e., including or excluding the content or categories according to consistently applied criteria of selection. This eliminates analysis in which only materials supporting the investigator's hypotheses are examined.
3. **Generality,** i.e., findings must have theoretical relevance. Purely descriptive information about content unrelated to other attributes of content or to the characteristics of the sender or recipient of the communication is of little scientific value.
4. **Quantification,** i.e., the answer of the question(s) raised should be in quantitative terms (Lasswell, Lerner and Pool, 1992). Some scholars (Kaplan and Goldsen, 1949) equate the term, 'quantitative' with 'numerical', i.e., classifying content in precise numerical terms. This means that inferences must be derived strictly from counts of 'frequency'. It also means that information should be conveyed as "40 people or 40 out of 100 people had this opinion", because it is more precise that the statement "less than half or a large number of people had this opinion".

But others (Lazarsfeld and Barton, 1951) say that 'qualitativeness' and quantitativeness' are not dichotomous attributes but fall along a continuum, i.e., inferences are drawn from combined frequency and non-frequency techniques. Despite the advantages of quantitative methods, the tendency to equate content analysis with tabulation of frequencies has been criticized on a number of grounds:

1. The most important argument is that such a restriction leads to bias in the selection of problems to be investigated. Undue emphasis is placed on precision at the cost of problem significance.
2. Other argument is that more meaningful inferences can be drawn by non-quantitative measures. Qualitative analysis is more superior in the problems of applied social science.
3. The proponents of qualitative techniques also question the assumption (of the proponents of quantitative techniques) that for purposes of inference, frequency of assertion is necessarily related to the importance of assumption. They (proponents of qualitative techniques) say that the single appearance or omission of an attribute in a document may be

of more significance than the relative frequency of other characteristics.

4. Whether stated explicitly or not, even the most rigorously quantitative study uses qualitative techniques at some stage in the research.

Steps in Content Analysis

According to Sarantakos (1998), content analysis involves the same steps as in other methods of research, namely, selection of the area of research, formulation of research topic, designing research, collecting data and analyzing data. The difference in content analysis and other methods lies only in the 'content' of each step.

In the selection of the research area, the topic can be one whose various aspects are discussed by the newspapers, magazines, books, TV serials, movies and the like, e.g., communal violence, match fixing, police excesses at police stations, caste conflicts, violence in movies and the like. Formulation of research topic involves explaining and operationalising the topic, selection of units, determining categories and formulating hypothesis. Research design aims at determining the size of sampling, method of collecting data and methods of checking reliability. Data collection involves counting frequencies, gathering information on the intensity of the units, determining significance of units and evaluating units and intensity of the statements. Lastly, the analysis and interpretation of data aims at giving inferences and conclusions (Ahuja, 2003).

Trends in Content Analysis

Content analysis has been more in use in research since the beginning of the twentieth century. During one century, this technique has gone through many phases. Gardner (1975) has pointed out the following trends in this research technique:

1. Increased use of content analysis. In fact, its frequency has geometrically increased.
2. Heightened concern for theoretical and methodological issues.
3. Application to a broader spectrum of problems.
4. Increased use for testing hypotheses as opposed to purely descriptive research.

5. Greater diversity in the materials studied. The disciplines that account for the use of this research technique are sociology, medical science, anthropology, psychology, political science, journalism and mass communication.
6. Use in conjunction with other techniques of social research.
7. Content analysis by means of computers.

Tabulation

Tabulation is the process of summarizing raw data and displaying it in compact form for further analysis. Analysis of data is made possible through tables. Therefore, preparing tables is a very important step. Tabulation may be by hand, mechanical, or electronic. The choice is made largely on the basis of the size and type of study, alternative costs, time pressures, and the availability of computers and computer programmes. If the number of questionnaire is small and their length short, hand tabulation is quite satisfactory.

Tables can be divided into: (i) Frequency tables, (ii) Response tables, (iii) Contingency table, (iv) Univariate table, (v) Bivariate tables, (vi) Statistical tables, and (vii) Time series tables.

Generally a research table has the following parts: (a) table number, (b) title of the table, (c) caption, (d) stub (row heading), (e) body, (f) head note, (g) foot note.

As a general rule the following steps are necessary in the preparation of table:

1. **Title of Table:** The table should be first given a brief, simple and clear title which may express the basis of classification.
2. **Columns and rows:** Each table should be prepared in just adequate number of columns and rows.
3. **Captions and Stubs:** The columns and rows should be given simple and clear captions and stubs.
4. **Ruling:** Columns and rows should be divided by means of thin or thick rulings.
5. **Arrangement of Items:** Comparable figures should be arranged side by side.

6. **Derivations:** These should be arranged in the column near the original data so that their presence may easily be noted.
7. **Size of Columns:** This should be according to requirement.
8. **Arrangement of Items:** This should be according to the problem.
9. **Special Emphasis:** This can be done by writing important data in bold or special letters.
10. **Unit of measurement:** The unit should be noted below the line.
11. **Approximation:** This should also be noted below the title.
12. **Foot notes:** These may be given below the table along with sources.
13. **Total:** Totals of each column and Grand total should be in one line.

It is not always necessary to present facts in tabular from if they can be presented more simply in the body of the text. Tabular presentation enables the reader to follow quickly than textual presentation. A table should not merely repeat information covered in the text. The same information should not, of course, be presented in tabular form and graphical form. Smaller and simpler tables may be presented in the text while the large and complex table may be placed at the end of the chapter or report (Saravanavel, 2009).

Analysis

By analysis it means the computation of certain indices or measures along with searching for patterns of relationship that exist among the data groups. Analysis, particularly in case of survey or experimental data, involves estimating the values of unknown parameters of the population and testing of hypotheses for drawing inferences.

Analysis may, therefore, be categorized as descriptive analysis and inferential analysis (Inferential analysis is often known as statistical analysis). "Descriptive analysis is largely the study of distributions of one variable. This study provides us with profiles of companies, work groups, persons and other subjects on any of a multiple of characteristics such as size, composition, efficiency, preferences, etc", (Emory, 1976). This sort of analysis may be in respect of one variable (described as unidimensional analysis), or in respect of two variables (described as bivariate analysis) or in respective of more than two variables (described as multivariate analysis). In this context the researcher works out various measures that show the size and shape of a distribution(s) along with the study of measuring relationship between two or more variables.

Analysis may include correlation analysis and causal analysis. Correlation analysis studies the joint variation of two or more variables for determining the amount of correlation between two or more variables. Causal analysis is concerned with the study of functional relationships existing between two or more variables. This analysis can be termed as regression analysis. Causal analysis is considered relatively more important in experimental researches, whereas in most social and business researches, interest lies in understanding and controlling relationships between variables than with determining causes per se and as such one consider correlation analysis as relatively important.

In modern times, with the availability of computer facilities, there has been rapid development of multivariate analysis which may be defined as "all statistical methods which simultaneously analyze more than two variables on a sample of observations", (Sheth, 1971). Usually the following analyses are involved when one makes a reference of multivariate analysis:

1. Multiple regression analysis: This analysis is adopted when the researcher has one dependent variable which is presumed to be a function of two or more independent variables. The objectives of this analysis is to make a prediction about the dependent variable based on its covariance with all the concerned independent variables.
2. Multiple discrimination analysis: This analysis is appropriate when the researcher has a single dependent variable that cannot be measured, but can be classified into two or more groups on the basis of some attributes. The object of this analysis happens to be to predict an entity's possibility of

belonging to a particular group based on several predictor variables.

3. Multivariate analysis of variance (or multi-ANOVA): This analysis is an extension of two way ANOVA, wherein the ratio of among group variance to within group variance is worked out on a set of variables.
4. Canonical Analysis: This analysis can be used in case of both measurable and non-measurable variables for the purpose of simultaneously predicting a set of dependent variables from their joint covariance with a set of independent variables.

Inferential analysis is concerned with various tests of significance for testing hypotheses in order to determine with what validity data can be said to indicate some conclusion or conclusions. It is also concerned with the estimation of population values. It is mainly on the basis of inferential analysis that the tasks of interpretation. (i.e., the task of drawing inferences and conclusions) is performed.

Statistics in Research

The role of statistics in research is to function as a tool in designing research, analyzing its data and drawing conclusions therefrom. Most research studies result in a large volume of raw data which must be suitably reduced so that the same can be read easily and can be used for further analysis. Clearly, the science of statistics cannot be ignored by any research worker, even though they may not have the occasion to use statistical methods in all their details and ramifications. Classification and tabulation, as stated earlier, achieve this objective to some extent, but one has to do a step further and develop certain indices or measures to summarize the collected / classified data. Only after this one can adopt the process of generalization from small groups (i.e., samples) to population.

In fact, there are two major areas of statistics viz., descriptive statistics and inferential statistics. Descriptive statistics concerns with the development of certain indices from the raw data, whereas inferential statistics concerns with the process of generalization. Inferential statistics are also known as sampling statistics and are mainly concerned with two major type of problems: (i) the estimation of population parameters and (ii) the testing of statistical hypotheses.

The important statistical measures that are used to summarize the survey / research data are:

(1) measures of central tendency or statistical average, (2) measures of dispersion, (3) measures of asymmetry (skewness); (4) measures of relationship; and (5) other measures.

Amongst the measures of central tendency, the three most important ones are the arithmetic average or mean, median and mode. Geometric mean and harmonic mean are also sometimes used. From among the measures of dispersion, variance, and its square root the standard deviation are the most often used measures. Other measures such as mean deviation, range, etc., are also used. For comparison purpose, mostly the coefficient of standard deviation or the coefficient of variation is used.

In respect of the measures of skewness and kurtosis, mostly use ones are, the first measure of skewness based on mean or median. Other measures of skewness, based on quartiles or on the methods of moments, are also used sometimes. Kurtosis is also used to measure the peakedness of the curve of the frequency distribution.

Amongst the measures of relationship, Karl Pearson's coefficient of correlation is the frequently used measure in case of statistics of variables, whereas Yule's coefficient of association is used in case of statistics of attributes.

Multiple correlation coefficient, partial correlation coefficient, regression analysis, etc., are other important measures often used by a researcher. Index numbers, analysis of time series, coefficient of contingency, etc., are other measures that may as well be used by a researcher, depending upon the nature of the problem under study (Kothari, 2009).

Frequency Distribution

The frequency distribution is a table in which all score units are listed in one column and the number of individuals receiving each score appears as frequencies in the second column (Geilford, 1965). The frequency distribution is a table in which all score units are listed in one column and the number of individuals receiving each score appears as frequencies in the second column:

Simple Frequency Distributions

When the score range is small (no more than 20 score units), these can be listed in simple rank order from highest to lowest in column one and the frequencies entered in column two:

Score	*f*
15	1
14	0
13	3
12	2
11	6
10	5
9	2
8	4
7	1
6	2
	N = 26

Grouped Frequency Distributions

When the score range is (more than 20 score units), these are grouped into a hierarchy of class intervals of equal width in column one and the corresponding frequencies in column two:

Class Interval	*f*	*Cum. f'*
42-44	3	120
39-41	11	117
36-38	8	106
33-35	23	98
30-32	35	75
27-29	14	40
24-26	10	26
21-23	9	16
18-20	6	7
15-17	1	1
		N= 120

Rules for constructing class intervals in a grouped frequency distribution:

1. In general, there should be between 10 and 20 class intervals based on the optimal number that will efficiently summarize the data without distorting its shape. Too few compresses the data, concealing meaningful changes in its shape; too many stretch out the data creating unnecessary gaps.
2. The width of the class interval is a function of the range of the raw scores and the number of class intervals desired. In the above example, if the raw score range was 49-17=32 and the researcher wanted about 10 class intervals, 32\10=3.20. Rounded to the nearest whole number, a class interval width of 3 is obtained.
3. In general, when the width of the class interval is less than 10 score units, odd number widths (1, 3, 5, 7, 9) are more

convenient since the midpoint of the interval will be a whole number. . For interval sizes of 10 and above, multiplies of 5 (10, 15, 20, etc.) are recommended.

4. "Real" versus "Apparent" limits for the class interval. In statistical calculations based on grouped data it is necessary to use the real limit (rather than the apparent limit) of a given class interval. For example, in the above grouped frequency distribution the interval 36-38 has apparent lower and upper limits of 36 and 38. Strictly speaking, however, the real lower and upper limits of the interval 36-38 are 35.5 and 38.5

Graph Representations of Data

(A) Histogram or Bar

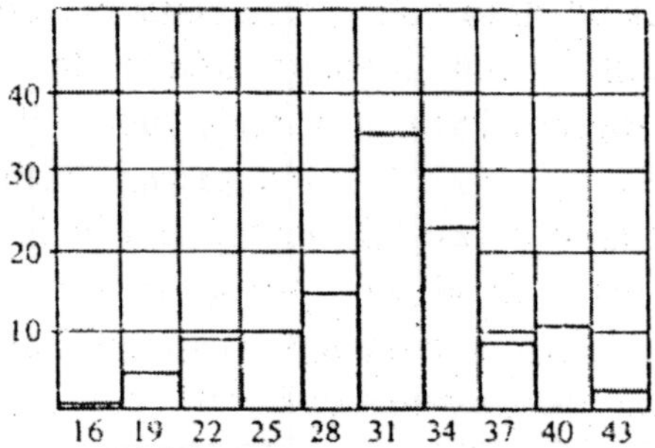

Scores
(Midpoint of class interval)

(A) Frequency Polygon

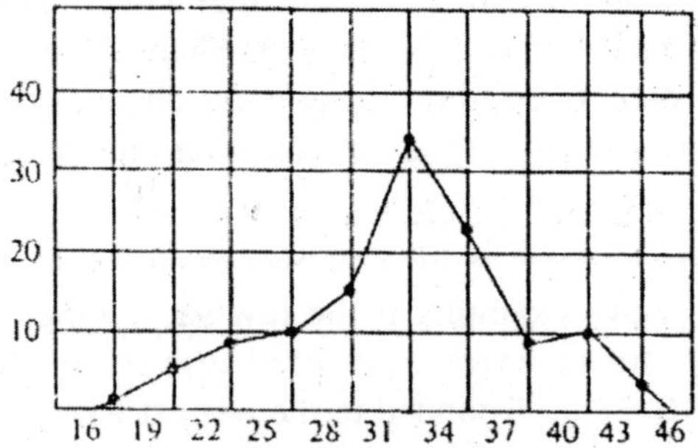

Scores
(Midpoint of class interval)

1. Histograms or bar graphs and frequency polygons are very similar, both being constructed from frequency distributions.
2. The scores are plotted along the horizontal baseline, also called the abscissa or X axis. The *frequencies* (number of percent of cases) are plotted along the vertical axis, also called the ordinate or Y axis.

(a) For the histogram or bar graph, the width of each base corresponds to the real limits of the width of each class interval. In the above example, this fact holds true although the midpoints of each class interval are presented for clearer reading. The height of each bar corresponds to the frequency or percent of cases in that interval.

(b) For the frequency polygon, the points are plotted directly over the midpoints of each class interval.

(c) For good graphic proportions, the vertical axis should be roughly two thirds the length of the horizontal axis.

(A) Cumulative Frequency Curve

1. Cumulative frequency curves represent the graphing of a cumulative distribution and plotted according to procedures similar to the frequency polygon.

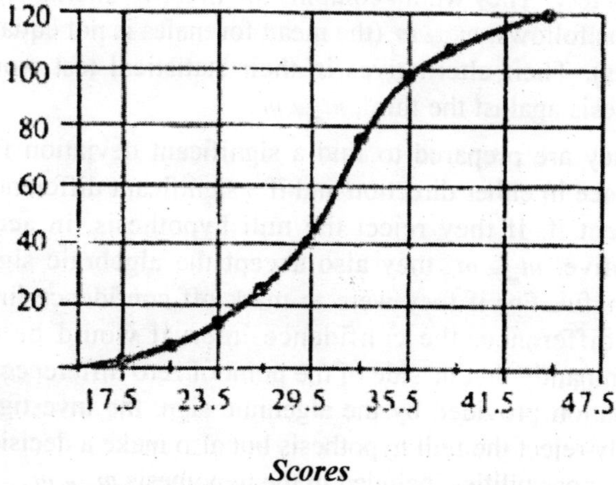

Scores

(Upper real limit of class interval)

1. Using the X and Y axes noted above, points are plotted directly above the upper real limit of each interval. This is necessary because the cumulative frequency represents the number of cases that have scores equal to or below the value at that particular upper limit.
2. Cumulative frequency curves are useful when we are primarily interested in determining the position of an individual in a group, rather than the general form of the group performance as in the case of the histogram or frequency polygon (Isaac & Michael, 1982).

Hypothesis Testing

Let it be that the hypotheses which are concerned have to do with a sex difference in verbal comprehension ability. Logically, there are three alternatives: (1) males have more ability than females; (2) females have more ability than males; or (3) there is no sex difference connected with this ability. In terms of symbols, these three alternatives may be expressed as follows: where the $m_m > m_{fl}$ $m_m < m_{fl}$ and $m_m = m_{fl}$ where then's stand for population means and the subscripts denote male and female.

Investigators who approach this problem with open minds simply ask, "Is there a genuine sex difference here?" They would make a two-tail test. They would combine the first two alternatives into one, stated as follows: $m_m \neq m_f$ (the mean for males is not equal to that for females). Their alternatives in their statistical test would be this hypothesis against the third, $m_m \neq m_f$.

They are prepared to find a significant deviation from a zero difference in either direction and if a significant difference is found, to accept it. If they reject the null hypothesis, in accepting the alternative, $m_m \neq m_{fl}$ they also accept the algebraic sign as being meaningful. For if they were to mark off confidence limits for the mean difference, the confidence interval would be entirely or predominantly on one side of the point of zero difference. Using the information provided by the algebraic sign, the investigators could not only reject the null hypothesis but also make a decision between the two possibilities included in the hypothesis $m_m \neq m_f$.

Investigators who think they have reason to favour the hypothesis

$m_m > m_f$ or the hypothesis $m_m < m_f$ on logical grounds, on the basis of previous experience, or both would make a one tail test. If they believe that females are superior to males in verbal comprehension ability, they will reduce the situation to two alternatives by making another kind of combination. That is, the hypothesis to be tested would be $m_m = m_f$; with the alternative hypothesis (which they expect to be true) $m_m < m_f$. They would expect a significant deviation in the negative direction in the distribution of the quantities $m_m - m_f$ about the hypothetical mean (of the distribution of difference between pairs of sample means) of zero.

In either, a one or a two tail test, the reduction of three alternative hypotheses to two is an important simplifying step that facilitates decision making. The two alternatives are often symbolized by H_o and H_a. Ho represents the hypothesis that is tested, and H_o is its alternative (Guilford and Fruchter, 1985).

Chi square

Chi square is used with data in the form of frequencies, or data that can be readily transformed into frequencies. This includes proportions and probabilities. One important feature of chi square is its additive property, which makes possible the combination of several statistics or other values in the same test. Thus, a hypothesis involving more than one set of data can be tested for significance.

Chi-square test

"*Chi-square test*" is also known as Pearson's chi-square test.

A Chi-square test (also chi-squared or χ^2 test) is any statistical hypothesis test in which the sampling distribution of the test statistic is a chi-square distribution when the null hypothesis is true, or any in which this is asymptotically true, meaning that the sampling distribution (if the null hypothesis is true) can be made to approximate a chi-square distribution as closely as desired by making the sample size large enough.

Some examples of chi-squared tests where the chi-square distribution is only approximately valid:

- **Person's chi-square test**, also known as the chi-square goodness-of-fit test or chi-square test for independence. When mentioned without any modifiers or without other precluding context, this test is usually understood (for an exact test used in place of χ^2, see Fisher's exact test).

- Yates' chi-square test, also known as Yates' correction for community.
- Mantel-Haenszel chi-square test.
- Linear-by-linear association chi-square test.
- The portmanteau test in time-series analysis, testing for the presence of auto correlation.
- Likelihood-ratio tests in general statistical modeling, for testing whether there is evidence of the need to move from a simple model to a more complicated one (where the simple model is nested within the complicated one).

One case where the distribution of the test statistic is an exact chi-square distribution is the test that the variance of a normally-distributed population has a given value based on a sample variance. Such a test is uncommon in practice because values of variances to test against are seldom known exactly.

Chi-square test for variance in a normal population

If a sample of size *n* is taken from a population having a normal distribution, then there is a well-known result which allows a test to be made of whether the variance of the population has a pre-determined value. For example, a manufacturing process might have been in stable condition for a long period, allowing a value for the variance to be determined essentially without error.

Suppose that a variant of the process is being tested, giving rise to a small sample of product items whose variation is to be tested. The test statistic *T* in this instance could be set to be the sum of squares about the sample mean, divided by the nominal value for the variance (i.e. the value to be tested as holding). Then *T* has a chi-square distribution with n-1 degrees of freedom. For example if the sample size is 21, the acceptance region fir *T* for a significance level of 5% is the interval 9.59 to 34.17.

(http/en.wikipedia.org/wiki/Chi-square_test.)

Chi-square distribution

In probability theory and statistics, the chi-square distribution (also chi-squared or χ^2-distribution) with x degrees of freedom is the distribution of a sum of the squares of k independent standard normal random variables. It is one of the most widely used probability distributions in inferential statistics, e.g., in hypothesis testing, or in construction of confidence intervals.

The best-known situations in which the chi-square distribution is used are the common chi-square tests for goodness of fit of an observed distribution to a theoretical one, and of the independence of two criteria of classification of qualitative data. Many other statistical tests also lead to a use of this distribution, like Friedman's analysis of variance by ranks.

The chi-square distribution is a special case of the gamma distribution.

9
INTERPRETATION AND RESEARCH WRITING

Interpretation

After collecting and analyzing the data, the researcher has to accomplish the task of drawing inferences followed by report writing. This has to be done very carefully; otherwise misleading conclusion may be drawn and the whole purpose of doing research may get vitiated. It is only through interpretation that the researcher can expose relations and processes that underline his findings. In case of hypotheses testing studies, if hypotheses are tested and upheld several times, the researcher may arrive at generalizations. But in case the researcher had no hypothesis to start with, he would try to explain his findings on the basis of some theory. This may at times result in new questions, leading to further research. All this analytical information and consequential inference(s) may well be communicated, preferably through research report, to the consumer of research results who may be either an individual or a group of individuals or some public / private organizations.

Meaning of Interpretation

Interpretation refers to the task of drawing inferences from the collected facts after an analytical and / or experimental study. In fact, it is a search for broader meaning of research findings. The task of interpretation has two major aspects viz., (i) the effort to establish continuity in research through linking the results of a given study with those of another and (ii) the establishment of some explanatory concepts. "In one sense, interpretation is concerned with relationships within the collected data, partially overlapping analysis. Interpretation also extends beyond the data of the study to include the results of other research, theory and hypotheses." (Emory, 1976) Thus, interpretation is the device through which the factors that seem to explain what has been observed by the researcher in the course of the study can be better understood and it also provides a theoretical conception which can serve as a guide for further researches. (Emory, 1976)

Why Interpretation?

Interpretation is essential for the simple reason that the usefulness and utility of research findings lie in proper interpretation. It is being considered a basic component of research process because of the following reasons:

1. It is through interpretation that the researcher can well understand the abstract principle that works beneath his findings. Through this he can link up his findings with those of other studies, having the same abstract principle and thereby can predict the concrete world of events. Fresh inquiries can test these predictions later on. This way the continuity in research can be maintained.
2. Interpretation leads to the establishment of explanatory concepts that can serve as a guide for future research studies; it opens new avenues of intellectual adventures and simulates the quest for more knowledge.
3. Researcher can better appreciate only through interpretation, why his findings are what they are and can make others to understand the real significance of his research findings.
4. The interpretation of the findings of exploratory research study often results into hypotheses for experimental research and as such interpretation is involved in the transition from exploratory to experimental research. Since an exploratory study does not have a hypothesis to start with, the findings of such a study have to be interpreted on a post-factum basis in which case the interpretation is technically described as 'post factum' interpretation.

Techniques in Interpretation

The task of interpretation is not an easy job, rather it requires a great skill and dexterity on the part of the researcher. Interpretation is an art that one learns through practice and experience. The researcher may, at times, seek the guidance from experts for accomplishing the task of interpretation.

The techniques of interpretation often involve the following steps:

1. Researcher must give reasonable explanations of the relations which he has found and he must interpret the lines of relationship in terms of the underlying processes and must try to find out the thread of uniformity that lies under the surface layer of his diversified research findings. In fact, this is the technique of how generalization should be done and concepts be formulated.
2. Extraneous information, if collected during the study, must be considered while interpreting the final results of research study, for it may prove to be a key factor in understanding the problem under consideration.
3. It is advisable, before embarking upon the final interpretation, to consult someone having an insight into the study and one who is frank and honest and will not hesitate to point out omissions and errors in logical argumentation. Such a consultation will result in correct interpretation and thus, will enhance the utility of research results.
4. Researcher must accomplish the task of interpretation only after considering all relevant factors affecting the problem to avoid false generalization. He must be in no hurry while interpreting results, for quite often the conclusions, which appear to be all right at the beginning, may not at all be accurate (Kothari, 2009).

Interpretation of Data

Interpretation brings in the broader meaning of research findings. This search has two major aspects. First, there is the effort to establish continuity in social research through linking the results of one study with those of another. Secondly, interpretation leads to the establishment of explanatory concepts. Through interpretation, the meanings and implications of the study become clear. Analysis is not complete without interpretation; and interpretation cannot proceed without analysis. Both are thus, inter-dependent. In fact, interpretation can be conceived of as a part of analysis. It is the task of interpretation to find out a link or a position of the study in the whole analytical framework. It connects the findings with the established theories or the available stock of knowledge in a particular area of research. Although, chronologically, analysis and interpretation occupy the last stage of the research process, they occupy the first stage, since the necessary theoretical and practical knowledge of the future shape of the result acquired much before the actual work is undertaken.

In view of the diversity of the research methods used in social sciences and the corresponding diversity of the data they seek, the interpretation of such data is best considered within the context of each of the methods. It calls for a critical examination of the results of one's analysis in the light of all the limitations of his data-gathering. It is a very important step in the total procedure of research.

Forms of Interpretation

It is an accepted creed that statistical data and information may be interpreted in various forms-depending on the size and nature of data and the need of its interpretation.

Some of the common and important forms or basis of interpretation may be described as:

1. ***Relationship:*** One of the most fundamental basis of interpretation is to find out the relationship. In general, it is seen that unless comparative analysis or study is made, true form of relationship between the subject and the object cannot be determined. On the contrary, unless true and proper relationships are established amongst 'different aspects', interpretation may never be considered as complete.

2. ***Proportion:*** Proportion is generally ascertained to determine the nature and form of absolute changes in the object of study. In particular, if the object of study is too much variable over a period, then proportions are ascertained to interpret the data or information in a true form.

3. ***Percentage:*** Sometimes the basis of interpretation is the percentage. If the object of enquiry is to determine the nature and extent of approximations only for a particular objective, then the method of percentage is often used for making

interpretation as the basis. In this regard we must keep in mind that although the method of percentage is somewhat crude and 'approximate', yet it is often used in the sphere of absolute figures.

4. *Average or other measures of comparison:* The method of averages or other measures of comparisons are used to interpret statistical data and information. It is a matter of common experience that if a long statistical table is to be analyzed and interpreted, we have to take the help of various forms of measuring the central or other tendencies relating to them. In the absence of these comparative measurements a definite and clear-cut result may not be arrived at. Therefore, averages or other measures of comparisons are considered to be not only desirable, but an essential and integral part of interpretation (Saravanavel, 2009).

Essential for Interpretation

Some of the pre-conditions or essentials of interpretation may be mentioned as follows,

1. *Accurate Data:* One of the most important pre-requisites of interpretation and analysis is the availability of accurate and reliable data. In the absence of such material, the investigator fails to interpret the data in a proper and required form. On the contrary, if the data is inaccurate, none can accept the validity of its value.
2. *Sufficient Data:* Another important pre-requisite of interpretation is the existence of sufficient and reliable data. The main reason of it is that unless one has sufficient data, he may never achieve the objectives of proper interpretation and analysis. For, some of the rules and methods are applicable only if there is sufficient data. In the absence of it, not only the law of inertia or that of large numbers is not applicable, but the analysis or interpretation may also fail to yield the desired result.
3. *Proper type of Classification and Tabulation:* For attaining the objective of interpretation, in most of the cases, the investigators are required to base their calculations, estimations

and judgments on data represented in a properly classified and tabulated form. It is a well-known fact that if a set of data and information is analyzed taking into account faulty and defective type of classification or tabulation, there is every possibility of committing errors or arriving at wrong conclusions.

4. *Absence of Heterogeneous Data:* For a uniform and accurate result, the data must be homogeneous. The reason is that if the data are non-homogeneous or heterogeneous, it may fail to yield the desired result. For in such cases the application of statistical methods is not only impeded, but may even fail to mould it to the proper channel.
5. *Possibility of Statistical Treatment:* In particular, if the subject concerned is related to 'quality' or if the information available is scanty, it may not be regarded as suitable for statistical treatment. While dealing with the important and useful aspect of interpretation and analysis, one has to keep a vigilant eye on the nature of enquiry as well as on the availability of data for conducive statistical treatment.
6. *Consistency of Information:* Inconsistent information and data are always subject to inaccurate results. In mathematical and statistical treatment, however, emphasis is always laid on having stable and accurate results. Therefore, for having a better standard of interpretation and results, it is always desirable that all statistical treatments should be subjected to consistent data and information. (Saravanavel, 2005)

Characteristics of a Good Research Report and Thesis

Presentation of research findings in the form of a report is a necessary part of the research process. The main purpose of report is to convey the whole result of the study in sufficient details, so that new findings or new methods of analysis can be incorporated into the general store of knowledge available in the area. A report is the detailed description of what has been done and how it has been done with respect to a particular area or topic of research. A report may also be addressed to the experts in the field for a critical examination of the achievements made, if any, for the purpose of keeping alive the spirit of enquiry. The purpose of a report is the dissipation of knowledge, broadcasting of generalization and helping further research in the related field. A research report may be helpful to throw some new lights which can make the building up of a new hypothesis and thus can make possible new theorizing (Ghosh, 1987).

While writing the research report it is very essential to keep in mind the level of knowledge of the readers. A report written for expert evaluators or scientists or a specialized institution must be more rigorous and more detailed than what is written for the general readers. There are various types of research reports. They are called by different names such as essay, assignment, term-paper, project report, study paper, professional paper, monograph, field book, dissertation, thesis etc.

Different Types of Reports

1. Term-Papers and Assignments

The term-paper is an academic report which may have one or several objectives. Generally it is based on a library investigation of some topic and rarely involves laboratory / field work. In institutions, where both opportunity and encouragement make it possible, the student may make a field study of a problem in one or more business firms. An intermediate level of investigation might be based on correspondence with business firms or small sample surveys which can be carried out conveniently in a semester (Saravanavel, 1994).

In the case of a literary project, the term-paper project may have the purpose of determining the state of art of a narrow subject, evaluating processes or institutions; organizing, classifying, and interpreting business data such as historical expenditures on advertising; or presenting and comparing view points of authorities on a topic. The term paper in such a case is primarily a record of literary search and intelligent analysis of reading on a single subject. The term-paper is short enough so that it does not require an appendix common to large expositions. Ten to thirty papers (typed in double spaced) covers the range of most papers. The term paper is used to acquaint the student with systematic, careful and accurate gathering and presentation of information. It is not supposed to be a series of a quotations tied together by an occasional linking sentence by the student.

Assignments and term-papers are announced well in advance or from time to time, as and when a relevant portion of the syllabus is taught. They serve as follow up to the actual teaching. Sometimes assignments are geared to cover important aspects of a subject not covered by lectures or tutorials, called "text-book assignments." However, in both the cases, some guidance may be given to the student in the form of suggested reading list. Assignments can be planned as exercises common for all students in a class. But these, usually lead to copying of one by another. In contrast, the differentiated assignments, where different tasks in subject matter are assigned to different students, become more instructive.

2. The Professional Paper

The professional paper is directed towards either a basic research problem or an applied research problem. The applied research report solves an operating problem for a particular company at a particular time. The professional paper, if it does this at all, is such that the problem is one which faces many companies and the solution presented may be adopted by those companies. The professional business papers as they appear in the journals vary considerably in purpose if a statement of the objective is given at the beginning. Business schools, which offer a course culminating in a professional paper, offer the student an opportunity to conduct a small research project to gain experience in research and report writing. The professor guiding these projects may be hazy about alternative organizations or may be dogmatically inclined toward the traditional, report or experiment. It may be wise to ask which type of organization is easiest for the business manager to read and advise the student of this alternative. That is, have the student organize, the report to give the answer first.

3. Research Monograph

The research monograph is a research report covering a fairly large research project on a single subject. It is usually a form of communication among scholars in a particular field, and as such, has a limited audience. Since the monograph is usually longer than an article but shorter than a book, publication of the research monograph is usually supported by a university press, a bureau of business research, a research foundation, or the author himself. The research monograph has historically been a very scholarly treatment of some aspect of theory, written by a single author. The monograph may be highly theoretical dealing with concepts, principles, ideas and procedural aspects of a topic of study. In contrast, a highly empirical study covers the results of investigating the capital-expenditure decision making process in large companies.

4. Dissertation and Thesis

The dissertation represents a species of essay different form the thesis. Its function is to provide systematic discussion on a subject or topic. The purpose of the dissertation is to establish an arguable view. To dissertate is to discourse, or argue, in a learned manner. A thesis is a detailed dissertation which maintains a valuable proposition or hypothesis, written on the basis of a detailed research. The dissertation as a requirement of post-graduate education represents the culmination of natural investigation of a relatively narrow and specific problem. In its narrowest sense, it has been considered the substantiation of a specific point of view. A thesis today commonly regarded as a coherent report of research, in which both the process and the results are given. Its origin is a problem, its central proposition is a hypothesis. A thesis include preliminary parts and reference sections, similar to the form of a book, differentiating it from a term-paper.

Dissertations and thesis are research project reports. Writing of such reports involves a critical and disciplined inquiry in a problem and presenting the result of such a critical enquiry according to accepted methods/procedures. A thesis is academically superior to a dissertation and is much more than a large term-paper. A thesis involves a more original research and is expected to make an original contribution to knowledge. Both a dissertation and a thesis, normally represent the culmination of a substantial piece of independent and original work over a stipulated period, under a recognized expert's guidance. Outside examiners are usually engaged to evaluate theses and dissertations before conferring the degree. When accepted, the thesis virtually becomes public property and thesis abstracts are published periodically. Standard set for thesis must, therefore, be much higher than those set for essays. (Ghosh, 1987)

The degree of originality expected is related to the level of the course, i.e., the more advanced the course, the more originality is expected. In undergraduate research project reports the student may be justified in presenting a synthesis of material drawn largely from secondary sources while at post-graduate level the student is expected to rely more on primary sources. The more advanced the course, the narrow and hence more specialized will be the field of research and greater will be the depth of reading and other investigations required. Now a days integrated research is gaining importance. The length of the research project report tends to increase in proportion to the originality requirements. The shortest one (under-graduate) will be about 4,000 words while a postgraduate report could extend to 6,000 or even up to 10,000 words.

At M. Phil., M. Litt., and Ph.D., levels the length of the report will be about 150 to 350 pages. However, the length is less important than quality and many excellent thesis are relatively short. Many faculty members believe that greater conciseness should be encouraged so that the doctoral thesis is kept considerably shorter. More faculty members could read it and criticize it, and the adviser would be able to read the report more often and more thoroughly. The result should lead to higher quality, and the scholar should derive more value from this experience.

Finally, as regards presentation, the more advanced the course, the greater attention the writer will have to pay to details, especially in documentation, e.g., quotations, foot notes, bibliography, appendices, etc., will have to be accurate. Whatever the level, however, the fundamental purposes of all research project works remains the same:

(a) to place more emphasis on the submission of written work, as part of normal course requirements, for purposes of student assessment,

(b) to liberate students from dependence upon course books and lectures, and

(c) to develop a student's ability to find, interpret and present material.

Style and Presentation

There is no unique and universally acceptable method of writing a research report. Much will depend on the topic of research, the degree of sophistication introduced, the type and extent of the materials and the techniques introduced, and above all, the argumental and the imagination of the researcher. In the matter of writing, no two researchers are alike so far as style and presentation schemes are concerned. A research report is essentially a scientific document, and hence it must be clear, accurate and precise. Confusion, ambiguity, pretentiousness and high sounding words must be carefully guarded against by a researcher. It is sometimes necessary to translate technicalities into language that would be understood by the readers. This is especially necessary when the report is meant for the general public. However, a report meant for experts may very well contain technicalities.

The very sensitive aspect of report is its language. The researcher should have an ideal language and style. He has to acquire them by experience, intuition, care and practice. Generally speaking, the emphasis should be on clarity, correct exposition, expression and simplicity. A very lengthy report may not be very scientific. A research scholar must essentially know a good bit of editing. He must have sufficient control over the language, its literature, grammar and composition. A style that is pleasing from a literary or aesthetic point of view is an additional quality of a researcher; but he has no obligation to be colorful or elegant in his writing.

The report should be free from subjective bias. The result should be objectively presented in a balanced way. Repetition of facts and statements are to be eliminated at any cost. The presentation of the facts must be logical. The relevant diagrams, graphs, tables and charts should be properly placed so that they become a part of the text where they are placed. They should have appropriate titles and dimensions. Tables and diagrams should be numbered, and where necessary, the sources of data should be specifically mentioned. The report should be presented in an attractive form i.e., typing should be accurate, neat and clean and with sufficient margins on all sides of the typed paper. The paper should be suitable for the purpose. The report must make use of sub-headings at appropriate places of discussion.

Footnotes or end notes are to be used in a report. They can be consecutively numbered. The books and journals cited in the footnotes or endnotes and in the bibliography should be highlighted. In the event of the publication they have to be printed in italics. Different abbreviations such as 'Ibid', 'Op. cit', and so on are used in the foot notes or endnotes. While writing footnotes or endnotes, the names of the articles/ research papers are kept within inverted commas. In book references, the name of the writer is followed by the name of his/her work, then comes the name of the publisher, place and year of publication and the relevant page number. In the case of articles, the name of the published journal and year and month of publication are to be mentioned. When there are many writers, one can use "et al" (others) after one author. There are two major ways of writing bibliography. They are APA style and MLA style. One should follow one style consistently.

Layout of the Research Report

The layout of the report means as to what the research report should contain. A comprehensive layout of the research report should comprise (A) preliminary pages; (B) the main text; and (C) the end matter.

1. Preliminary Pages

In its preliminary pages the report should carry a title and date, followed by acknowledgements in the form of 'Preface' or 'Foreword'. Then there should be a table of contents followed by a list of tables and illustrations so that the decision-maker or anybody interested in reading the report can easily locate the required information in the report.

2. Main Text

The main text provides the complete outline of the research report along with all details. Title of the research study is repeated at the top of the first page of the main text and then follows the other details on pages numbered consecutively, beginning with the second page. Each main section of the report should begin on a new page. The main text of the report should have the following sections: (i) Introduction; (ii) Statement of findings and recommendations; (iii) The results; (iv) The implications drawn from the results; and (v) The summary.

(a) **Introduction:** The purpose of introduction is to introduce the research project to the readers. It should contain a clear statement of the objectives of research i.e., enough background should be given to make clear to the reader why the problem was considered worth investigating. A brief summary of other relevant research may also be stated so that the present study can be seen in that context. The hypotheses of study, if any, and the definitions of the major concepts employed in the study should be explicitly stated in the introduction of the report.

The methodology adopted in conducting the study must be fully explained. The scientific reader would like to know in detail about: How was the study carried out? What was its basic design? If the study was an experimental one, then what were the experimental design? If the data were collected by means of questionnaires or interviews, then exactly what questions were asked? (The questionnaire or interview schedule is usually given in an appendix). If measurements were based on observation, then what instructions were given to the observers? Regarding the sample used in the study the reader should be informed: Who were the subjects? How many were there? How were they selected? All these questions are crucial for estimating the probable limits of generalizability of the findings. The statistical analysis adopted must also be clearly stated. In addition to all this, the scope of the study should be stated and the boundary lines be demarcated. Various limitations, under which the research project was completed, must also be narrated.

(b) **Statement of Findings and Recommendations:** After the introduction, the research report must contain a statement of findings and recommendations in non-technical language so that it can be easily understood by all concerned. If the findings happen to be extensive, at this point they should be put in the summarized form.

(c) **Results:** A detailed presentation of the findings of the study, with supporting data in the form of tables and charts together with a validation of results, is the next step in writing the main text of the report. This generally comprises the main body of the report, extending over several chapters. The result section of the report should contain statistical summaries and reductions of the data rather than the raw data. All the results should be presented in logical sequence and splitted into readily identifiable sections. All relevant results must find a place in the report. But how one is to decide about what is relevant, is the basic question. Quite often guidance comes primarily from the research problem and from the hypotheses, if any, with which the study was concerned. But ultimately the researcher must rely on his own judgment in deciding the outline of his report. "Nevertheless, it is still necessary that he states clearly the problem with which he was concerned, the procedure by which he worked on the problem, the conclusions at which he arrived, and the bases for his conclusions."

(d) **Implications of the Results:** Towards the end of the main text, the researcher should again put down the results of his research clearly and precisely. He should state the implications that flow from the results of the study, for the general reader is interested in the implications for understanding the human behavior. Such implications may have the following three aspects as stated below:

(i) A statement of the inferences drawn from the present study which may be expected to apply in similar circumstances.

(ii) The conditions of the present study which may limit the extent of legitimate generalizations of the inference drawn from the study.

(iii) The relevant questions that still remain unanswered or new questions raised by the study along with suggestions for the kind of research that would provide answers for them.

It is considered a good practice to finish the report with a short conclusion which summarizes and recapitulates the main points of the study. The conclusion drawn from the study should be clearly related to the hypotheses that were stated in the introductory section. At the same time, probable future perspectives and an indication of the kind of research which needs to be done in that particular field is useful and desirable.

(e) **Summary:** It has become customary to conclude the research report with a very brief summary, resting in brief the research problem, the methodology, the major findings and the major conclusions drawn from the research results.

3. End Matter

At the end of the report, appendices should be enlisted in respect of all technical data such as questionnaires, sample information, mathematical derivations and the like. Bibliography of sources consulted should also be given. Index (an alphabetical listing of names, places and topics along with the numbers of the pages in a book or report on which they are mentioned or discussed) should invariably be given at the end of the report. The value of index lies in the fact that it works as a guide to the reader for the contents in the report, (C.R. Kothari, 2009).

Structure of Research Report

Generally, a research report, whether it be called a dissertation or thesis, consists of three parts namely The Preliminary pages, The Text (the main body of the report), and the Reference Material.

I. Preliminary Section

The preliminaries consist of the following components:

1. the title page,
2. preface including acknowledgements,
3. table of contents,
4. list of tables,
5. list of figures (and illustrations), and
6. list of abbreviations

II. Text or Context

The Text of a dissertation / thesis consists of the following sections

1. Introduction (Introductory chapters),
2. Main body of the report (usually divided into chapters and sections), and
3. Conclusion (Summary, Recommendations / Suggestions).

III. Reference Material

The reference material is generally divided as follows:

1. Bibliography,
2. Appendice(s),/appendix
3. Glossary of Terms (if any), and
4. Index (if any).

Research report is considered a major component of the research study, for the research task remains incomplete till the report has been presented and / or written. As a matter of fact even the most brilliant hypothesis, highly well designed and conducted research study, and the most striking generalizations and findings are of little value unless they are effectively communicated to others. The purpose of research is not well served unless the findings are made known to others. Research results must invariably enter the general store of knowledge. All this explains the significance of writing the research report. There are people who do not consider writing of report as an integral part of the research process. But the general opinion is in favor of treating the presentation of research results or the writing of report as part and parcel of the research report. Writing of report is the last step in a research study and requires a set of skills somewhat different from those called for in respect of the earlier stages of research. This task should be accomplished by the researcher with utmost care; he may seek the assistance and guidance of experts for the purpose.

Guidelines for Planning, Preparing, Writing a Research

Proposal, Report, Thesis

The final and most important question asked of a research or evaluation study is "what does it meant"? Each previous section has contributed to the foundation on which the conclusions must rest. Careful planning, designing, instrumentation and statistical analysis form a composite prerequisite to reaching sound conclusions. Criteria and guidelines are included to assist the researcher in planning, preparing, writing and evaluating the research proposal, report, thesis (dissertation) or professional journal or article.

A Research Proposal: Checklist of Items for Possible Inclusion

Chapter I. The Problems

______ Introduction

______ Background of the problem (e.g., educational trends related to the problem, unresolved issues, social concerns)

______ Statement of the problem situation (basic difficulty – area of concern, felt need)

______ Purpose of the study (goal oriented) – emphasizing practical outcomes or products

______ Questions to be answered or objectives to be investigated

______ Definition of terms (largely conceptual here; operational definitions may follow in Methodology Chapter)

______ Rationale and theoretical framework (when appropriate)

______ Delineation of the research problem (explication of relationships among variables or comparisons to be considered)

______ Statement of hypotheses (conceptual rendition subsequently followed by operational statements in Chapter I or in Methodology Chapter)

______ Importance of the study – may overlap with statement of problem situation concepts

______ Scope and delimitations of the study (narrowing of focus)

______ Outline of the remainder of the thesis or proposal

Chapter II. Review of Literature

______ Organization of the present chapter – overview

______ Historical background (if necessary)

______ Purpose to be Served by Review of Research Literature

______ Acquaint reader with existing studies relative to what has been found,

______ who has done work, when and where latest research studies were completed, and what approaches involving research methodology, instrumentation, and statistical analyses were followed (literature review of methodology sometimes covered in first chapter and methodology)

______ Establish possible need for study and likelihood for obtaining meaningful, relevant and significant results

______ Furnish from delineation of various theoretical positions a conceptual framework affording bases for generation of hypotheses and statement of their rationale (when appropriate)

Note: In some highly theoretical studies the chapter "Review of Literature" may need to precede "The Problem" chapter so that the theoretical framework is established for a succinct statement of the research problem and hypotheses. In such a case, an advance organizer in the form of a brief general statement of the purpose of the entire investigation should come right at the beginning of the "Review of Literature" chapter.

Sources for Literature Review

______ General integrative reviews cited that relate to the problem situation or research problem such as those found in Review of Educational Research, Encyclopedia of Educational Research, or Psychological Bulletin.

______ Specific books, monographs, bulletins, reports and research articles – preference shown in most instances for literature of the last ten years.

______ Unpublished materials (e.g., dissertation, thesis, papers presented at recent professional meetings not yet published for, but possibly available through ERIC)

______ Selection and arrangement of literature review often in terms of questions to be considered, hypotheses set forth, or objectives or specific purposes delineated in problem chapter

______ Summary of literature reviewed (very brief)

Chapter III. Methodology of Procedures

______ Overview (optional)

______ Description of research methodology or approach (e.g., experimental, quasi-experimental, correlational, causal-comparative, or survey)

_______ Research design (Spell out independent, dependent and classificatory variables and sometimes formulate an operational statement of the research hypothesis in null form so as to set the stage for an appropriate research design permitting statistical inferences.)

_______ Pilot studies (as they apply to the research design, development of instruments, data collection techniques and characteristics of the sample)

_______ Selection of subjects (this is concerned with sample and population.)

_______ Field, class room or laboratory procedures (eg. instructions to subjects or distribution of materials)

_______ Data collection and recording

_______ Data processing and analysis (statistical analysis)

_______ Methodological assumptions

_______ Limitations (weaknesses)

_______ Possible restatement of conceptual hypotheses from problem chapter in operational form relative to instrumentation and experimental procedure or design followed (operationally stated hypotheses from problem chapter in operational form relative to instrumentation and experimental procedure or design followed (operationally stated hypotheses amenable to statistical testing)-if not done elsewhere.

_______ Summary (optional)

Chapter IV. Findings (Analysis and Evaluation)

_______ Findings are presented in tables or charts whenever appropriate and interpreted

_______ Analysis reported with respect to furnishing evidence for each question asked or each hypothesis posed in problem statement

_______ Appropriate headings are established to correspond to each main question or hypotheses considered

_____ Factual information kept separate from interpretation, inference and evaluation (one section for findings and one section for interpretation or discussion)

Note: In certain historical, case study and anthropological investigations, factual and interpretive material may need to be interwoven to sustain interest level, although the text should clearly reveal what is fact and what is interpretation.

______ Separate section often entitled "Discussion," "Interpretation," or "Evaluation" ties together findings in relation to theory, review of literature, or rationale

______ Summary of chapter

Chapter V. Findings Summary, Conclusion and Recommendation

______ Brief summary of everything covered in first four chapters highlighting of portion of Chapter IV

______ Conclusions ("so what" of findings; often the hypotheses restated as inferences with some degree of definitive commitment and generalisability)

______ Recommendations (practical suggestions for implementation of findings or for additional research)

(Joan, 1967).

Research Proposal Format

- **Title:** The Title of the project should be concise (with sub-title, if any) reflecting the scope of the investigation.
- **Aim of the Project:** The broad aim of the project emphasizing the overall thrust of the proposed investigation should be clearly mentioned.
- **Statement of the Problem:** The problem to be investigated should be clearly contextualized in the theoretical framework of the discipline.
- **Over view of Literature:** The Problem identified should be logically linked to other studies on the theme in the literature delineating the need for the present investigation.
- **Conceptual Framework:** The concepts to be used, their

relevance and applicability to the study and their operationalisation should be indicated.

- **Research Questions or Hypotheses:** The research questions to be answered / addressed need to be unequivocally stated.

- **Research Methodology**

(a) **Coverage:** The proposal should clearly indicate the universe of the study, sampling frame, sampling methods, sampling size, units of observation etc.

(b) **Data Collection:** The proposal should indicate sources of data, types of data, tools and techniques for collection of various categories of proposed data.

(c) **Data Analysis:** It should indicate the statistical techniques, if any, proposed to be used in data processing, specific packages for data analysis, content analysis, indices/scaling techniques proposed to be used, etc.,

- **Implications:** The proposal should state whether this research would bring forth any implications. For policy making either for the region concerned or the country, any methodological innovations contribute to theory building.

- **References:** The proposal should include a 'List of References' mentioned in the text along with other important recent additions to the literature on the theme. The references should indicate the author, place of publication, title, publisher and year of publication.

- **Duration of the Project:** The **duration** of the project can be estimated depending upon the scope and size of the project but **should not exceed two years**. It should indicate the time needed for various tasks such as preparation of schedules, pilot study (if any), data collection, data analysis, report writing, etc.

- **Personnel:** It should indicate the number and category of personnel needed for various tasks, their qualifications and the man-months needed with adequate justification.

- **Budget:** This should indicate the cost of personnel, travel (no. of days and place's with justification), data processing, stationery and printing, books, journals, equipment, contingency and any other items.

- **Summary: Five copies** of Summary of the Research Proposal (about 500 words) indicating the statements of the problem, objective of the study, research questions or hypotheses or both, sample size (if any) and research methodology should be provided. N. B. (Note that all the documents should be typed or word processed (font: Tohima. Size 12 point), single-sided, one and a half space on A-4(8" x 11" or 21.5 cm x 28 cm) white paper. The length of the research proposal should not exceed eight pages and that of the bio data two pages.)

(KSSR Format 2009)

Research and Development Perspectives in India: An Integrated Approach

Since independence, India has established a large number of national laboratories dealing with a variety of areas in Science and Technology (S&T) including agriculture and medicine. A number of institutions are also involved in research in social sciences and management studies. There are several agencies and departments of the government such as Council of Scientific and Industrial Research (CSIR), Department of Bio – Technology (DBT), Indian Council of Agricultural Research (ICAR), Indian Council of Medical Research (ICMR), Departments of Electronics (DOE), Department of Science and Technology (DST), etc. dealing with science and technology. In order to support social sciences and humanities, several councils such as the Indian Council of Social Science Research (ICSSR), Indian Council of Historical Research (ICHR), have been established. Goldman Achs predictions show that by 2025 India will be the third largest economy after China and USA.

In 1997, on the occasion of the 50th anniversary of our independence, the then President of India mentioned that our adherence to a democratic system of governance and our becoming self–sufficient in food production are the twin great achievements of the first fifty years of freedom from colonialism. On August 15, 2007, our Indian President was in a position to add that freedom from hunger and acute deprivation were also achievements of independent India. This is politically, economically and technologically feasible. The right to food is also the first among the Millennium Development goals of the United Nations. Harnessing science and technology for making the concept of "food, health, work and education for all" come true, has to be the bottom line of our research and development policies and priorities. As per the committee appointed by the MHRD under his chairmanship, which recently submitted its report on "Revitalizing Technical Education", over 30,000 Ph.Ds. are required to meet teaching requirements of the existing technical institutions alone. Mediocrity in our educational system can only multiply mediocrity and cannot create well qualified and knowledgeable innovators and scientists required by the country. Unless the valuable suggestions made above are followed up, India's hope of becoming an advanced nation will remain a dream. If, on the other hand, we back up our dream with concrete actions, India can indeed become a developed nation by 2020.

Emphasis on Over Specializations: Need to keep oneself aware of other Development to link Specialization with other Sectors

Nobel Laureate Hard observed at the Science Congress in Chandigarh that Indian Scientists end up being specialists only and in this process miss out on major discoveries. He remarked that "Scientists here need to expand their horizon and broaden their outlook. By concentrating only on their respective fields, they remain ignorant of what is going on in other related streams. Knowledge and awareness of other fields are indispensable for achieving breakthroughs and discoveries."

Some of the main problems related to R&D in our higher educational institutions are:

1. Most of the efforts are concentrated in a few institutions and not spread over the entire system. This should be seen in the context of the need to grow R&D culture in all institutions and at the same time using selectivity for creating and supporting groups of excellence.
2. Experimental scientists and engineers have the greatest handicap in the educational sector due to poor infrastructure

facilities. Maintenance, running cost, and technical support are not adequately provided for. Instrumentation is generally poor in the educational institutions.

3. An atmosphere and pace appropriate to research is difficult to sustain in the face of cumbersome rules, procedural difficulties and, most of all, lack of resources.

4. Cooperation and collaboration between research centers located in universities with R&D laboratories is scarce.

5. There is little premium on quality excellence especially in the area of relevant research and development. An appropriate system for recognizing excellence and appropriate system and rewarding performance is yet to evolve. While we have a number of scientists and engineers engaged in R&D and many more are needed, the aspect of quality requires greater emphasis.

6. Mediocrity in R&D has to be guarded against. Research is by and large confined to traditional areas; inter disciplinarity has not taken root. Choice of research problems is often dictated by considerations of easy publication in journals.

7. Even in otherwise well-equipped laboratories adequate provision for spares, consumables and replacement of short lived equipment is not available. Overheads need to be provided to the institutions by agencies sponsoring research. Without such overheads the institutions find it difficult to support research.

8. Poor library, inadequate information system and absence of computational and reprographic facilities are endemic to the majority of educational institutions. The need for modernization and removal of obsolescence in research facilities is urgent.

9. Research in Technology suffers due to lack of appropriate linkages, the absence of articulation of felt needs by the used industry, and by the absence of a strong linkage with basic science which provide primary inputs to technology. Research in technology is meager because highly qualified technical personnel find other avenues of employment more profitable.

10. Very little research is undertaken to improve existing technology or applying existing or newer technologies to meeting the needs of villages and rural areas. Generally, technologies which increase productivity and improve the performance of an existing process are not being developed. Imported technologies have not been suitably adapted to local situation.

11. Transfer / extension of technology even when developed indigenously, does not receive sufficient attention. A management culture suited for research and development of technology needs to be developed.

12. Scarce resources and facilities existing in some research organizations are not easily available for utilization by other organizations. There is a need for greater accessibility and cooperation.

13. The mechanisms for technology watching, technology assessment and technology forecasting need to be fully established and strengthened for providing guidance to the research worker on the one hand and the developmental agencies on the other to enable them to take suitable decision for providing funding and organizational support.

14. Industries as well as some S&T agencies draw heavily on the academic sector for their manpower needs yet they do not do enough financially or otherwise, to support R&D manpower development and / or research in the academic sector.

15. Linkage between research activity and the improvement of educational processes is very weak. Research will have to be utilized for renovation and renewal of the educational process and energizing modernization of curriculum. There is an absence of a modal agency for managing, implementing and monitoring R&D in education sector.

16. The results of social sciences research are not disseminated adequately to the policy makers in a form that they could be used in policy for mutation. The linkage between research and curriculum renewal is also weak.

17. Most of the researches in social science are uni - disciplinary. Inter integrated disciplinary and trans disciplinary researches are not taken up sufficiently. This is particularly needed in order to interface social sciences and humanities with Science and Technology.
18. The present recruitment practices in the Universities and other higher education institutions promote inbreeding. This requires immediate change.

    (University News 2009)

10

REFERENCE MATERIALS

Internet Search Service for Academic Research

Google Scholar Contents

The Google Scholar allows the researchers to specifically search for the academic contents on the Internet, which may be theses, books, technical reports and the peer reviewed research articles from broad areas of research and learning. It also includes preprints and the scholarly articles found on the Internet. Google Scholar sources its contents from Association for Computing Machinery (ACM), Institution of Electrical and Electronics Engineers (IEEE), Open form Online Computer Library Centre (OCLC), the open web and lot of other academic publishers it has working arrangements with (Sullivan, 2004). Some of these contents were not available on the Internet before because of the subscription restriction. It means some of the contents made available for search on the Google Scholar are unique too.

Search Service

Search Engine vs. Search Service

One uses a search engine like 'Google', 'Yahoo' or 'AltaVista' to find the information and documents on the Internet through a browser software like 'Internet Explorer', 'Firefox', 'Netscape Navigator' or 'Mozilla' on his computer. Authors prefer to use the term 'search service' in preference to the term 'search engine' in this communication. The search service should refer to whole of the hardware, software, technologies, procedures and the human, financial and connectivity infrastructure maintained to support the search by the services provider like Google while the search engine is only the software that searches its index for the search-terms in the search statement. The term search service is thus inclusive and a superset of the term search engine. This communication refers to the search service in this broader scope and context inclusive of its search engine.

Search Index

Search services maintain index of the search words in the contents available on the Internet. A software called spider or crawler creates this index by visiting all the web sites at the Internet through its interconnections. This process is termed as spidering or crawling of the Internet and the Google is not different in this respect. The index is periodically updated by revisiting the Internet at regular intervals (Bharat and Pateria, 2003).

Google's Scholarly Subset

The Google Scholar actually searches a scholarly subset of the main Google index, which consists of the documents identified as scholarly by an undisclosed Google algorithm. Since the Google Scholar searches only the scholarly subset of the Google index it has been successful in clearing the clutter of non-academic contents in the search.

Latency of the Index

When one searches the Internet, through a search engine, the search engine really searches its index and not the Internet. The Google Scholar does the same. This introduces a factor of latency in the Internet search results due to the latency of the search index maintained by the search service. The searches should be aware of the fact that some of the articles made available recently might not be found in the search result. Similarly, a document altered/improved or relocated recently may still have its older version or older URL address. Fortunately, the scholarly documents like peer reviewed research articles, technical reports or thesis etc., are rarely altered once published.

Search Interface

Simple Search Interface

The default search interface (the webpage and its search textbox) at http://scholar.google.com is simple, clean and straightforward. It has no clutter of distracting commercial, glamorous and sensational information diverting attention and carries no annoying advertisements unlike most other search engine interfaces. For the search just type the search term(s) in the search text box and press the <ENTER> key or click on 'Search' button. All of the Boolean or math's operators can be used for writing the complex search statements. Like Google the search operators are required to be capitalized and the 'AND' is the default Boolean operator between multiple search terms in a search statement unless an 'OR' or 'NOT' operator is specified between them. Google Scholar also has three field selection operators for limiting the search to certain fields of the document. To search, use 'intitle:' for a single term and 'alliantitle:' for all the multiple terms following the operator. To find papers/articles of a specified author the operator 'author' is used. Similarly to search only the URL address of a website for certain terms use the operator 'inurl:' the operators precede the search term and the colon ':' after all these are operators mandatory (Google Scholar help).

Efficiency of Simple Search

The Authors have found that even in the simple search interface, for a broad range of simple and complex scholarly search queries, the Google Scholar rejects more than 99.9 per cent of the material (assumed nonacademic) found on the Internet through several general-purpose search engines including the Google. Increasing the relevant documents in the search results by more than one thousand times is extra ordinarily efficient. This alone should make Google Scholar favorite of research scholars for their scholarly searches on the Internet in comparison to any other general-purpose search engine. This is perhaps the most important reason for the immediate uptake of the service immediately after its start while the speed of search may be the next one.

Advanced Search Interface

Click on 'Advanced Search' button of the simple search interface or use the URL http://scholar.google.com/advanced_scholar_search for the advanced search interface of the Google Scholar. The 'Advanced Search' provides for several fill in template fields, which are as follows:

1. In the template field 'with all of the words' type in the words that must necessarily occur in the documents required. It is equivalent to joining all the words in the field by the Boolean operator 'AND'.
2. In the field 'with the exact phrase' type in the exact phrase that the documents searched for must have. The words in this field are all treated as the words enclosed in the quote marks (" ") i.e., as one phrase,
3. In the field 'with at least one of the words' type in the words, at least one of which must occur in the documents required. It is equivalent to writing the Boolean operator 'OR' between all the words and enclosing them all in parenthesis,
4. In the field 'without the words', fill in the words that should not occur in the documents you are searching for. This is same as the use of Boolean operator 'NOT' before each of the words in this field,
5. In the field 'where my words occur' select the option 'in the title of the article' if you want to restrict the search only to the titles of the articles. Selection of the option 'anywhere in the article' searches the whole of the article including the title and this option is the default option.

The advanced interface also has three more fields 'Author', 'Publication' and 'Date', restricting the search only to the articles of some author, published in a journal and published between the years. The advanced search interface now also provides a check box field to restrict the search to any one or more of the seven subject areas. Fill in the last name of an author in the author field to search only for the documents authored by that specific author. To search for the articles only from a specific publication, type in its name in the publication field. To restrict the search to the documents published between the specified years, fill in the years in the 'Date' fields.

To find the articles only from any one or more of the selected seven broad subject (disciplinary) areas of research check mark the relevant check box(es), which are:

1. Biology, Life Sciences and Environment Science;
2. Business, Administration, Finance and Economics;

3. Chemistry and Materials Science;
4. Engineering, Computer Science and Mathematics;
5. Medicine, Pharmacology and Veterinary Science
6. Physics, Astronomy and Planetary Science; and
7. Social Sciences, Arts, Humanities.

The check marking of a subject area removes a lot of unwanted references from the other subject areas of research in the search results. The authors found that this rejects 50 to 99 per cent of the references from other subject areas saving as much of the time and efforts rejecting those references from the search results otherwise.

Together, all the Boolean, text and selection operators, provide a way to formulate a more precise search statement, extremely useful to get more of the relevant references in the search results. Saving of the time in searching (rejecting irrelevant results) allows a scholar to spend more time researching. Most scholars have limited time at their command and therefore, this can be a very important criteria for preferring one search service over the other.

Citing Electronic Publications

Citations of electronic sources and those of print sources should accomplish the same ends and have analogous formats. Both types of citations identify a source and give sufficient information to allow a reader to locate it. Yet each type requires a different kind and amount of information to fulfill these objectives. Print culture has developed standard reference tools (library catalogs, bibliographies, and so on) for locating published works.

Electronic media, in contrast, so far lack agreed-on means of organizing works. Moreover, electronic texts are not as fixed and stable as their print counterparts. Reference to electronic works therefore must provide more information that print citations generally on (Gibaldi 2000).

Publication Dates

Most bibliographic references to printed works contain only one date of publication; rare exceptions are an article reprinted in a collection of essays and a republished book. A citation of an electronic work, however, may require two and sometimes more publication dates to be identified fully. Since electronic texts can be readily altered, any accessed version of an online source is potentially different from any past or future version and therefore must be considered unique. Typically, then, a citation for an online text contains the date assigned to the document in the source as well as the date on which the researcher accessed the document. If the work originally had a print existence, it may be necessary to give the date of the original print publication, if provided, along with the date of electronic publication and the date of access, for the document may have been different at each stage.

Uniform Resource Locator (URL)

The most efficient way to find an online publication through its network address is through Uniform Resource Locator (URL). Since addresses can change, however, and their length and complexity can result in transcription errors, it is crucial to be as accurate as possible in supplying not only URLs but also other identifying information (e.g., author's name, title), so that the reader who cannot locate the material through the stated address might be able to find it with a network searching tool.

Moreover, since Internet sites and resources sometimes disappear altogether, one should consider downloading or printing the material he uses so that he can verify it if it is inaccessible later. Enclose URLs in angle brackets. If a URL must be divided between two lines, break it only after a slash; do not introduce a hyphen at the break or allow the word-processing program to do so.

Give the complete address, including the access mode identifier (http, ftp, gopher, telnet, news) and, after the first single slash, any relevant path and file names:

<http: / / www.princeton.edu/~lancelot/>

The recommendations in this section largely tend to treat sources for which a considerable amount of relevant publication information is available. In truth, though, many sources do not supply all desired information, for few standards currently govern the presentation of electronic publications; for instance, many texts do not include reference markers, such as paragraph numbers, so it is impossible to direct a reader to the exact location of the material he is citing. Thus, while aiming for comprehensiveness, writers must often settle for citing whatever information is available to them.

An Online Book

The typical entry for a complete online book available independently consists of the following items:

1. Author's name (if given). If only an editor, a compiler, or a translator is identified, cite that person's name, followed by the appropriate abbreviation (ed., comp., trans).
2. Title of the work (high lighted)
3. Name of the editor, compiler, or translator (if relevant).
4. Publication information. If the version of the text online has not been published before, give the date of electronic publication and the name of any sponsoring institution or organization. State the publication facts about the original print version if they are given in the source (e.g., city of publication, name of publisher, year of publication). Add in brackets relevant information not stated in the source.
5. Date of access and network address e.g., Austen, **Jane. Pride and Prejudice**. Ed. Henry Churchyard. 1996. 10 Sept. 1998 <http:// www.pemberley. com/janeinfo/pridprej.html>. Barsky, Robert F. **Noam Chomsky: A life of Dissent**. Cambridge: MIT P. 1997. 8 May 1998 http://mitpress.mit. edu/e-books/Chomsky/>.

An Article in an Online Periodical

Online Periodical publications include scholarly journals, newspapers, and magazines; works and other materials within such publications include articles, reviews, editorials, and letters to the editor. The typical entry for a work in an online periodical consists of the following items:

1. Author's name (if given).
2. Title of the work or material (if any; a review or letter to the editor may be untitled,) in quotation marks.
3. Name of the periodical (underlined).
4. Volume Number, issue number, or other identifying number.

5. Date of publication.
6. The number, range or total number of pages, paragraphs, or other sections, if they are numbered.
7. Date of access and network address e.g., Calabrese, Michael. "Between Despair and Ecstasy: Marco Polo's Life of the Buddha." **Exemplaria** 9.1 (1997). 22 June 1998 <http://web.english.ufl.edu/English/exemplaria/ calax.htm>. Denning, Peter J. "Business Designs for the New University." **Educom Review** 31.6 (1996). 23 June 1998.

   <http://educom.edu/web/pubs/review/review Articles/ 31620.html>

(Gibaldi 2000)

A Publication on CD-ROM, Diskette, or Magnetic Tape

Citations for publications on CD-ROM, diskette, and magnetic tape are similar to those for print sources, with the following important differences.

Publication Medium: Many works are published in more than one format (e.g., print, online, CD-ROM), and the works may not be the same in each. When one cites a publication on CD-ROM, diskette, or magnetic tape, it is important to state the publication medium in order to differentiate the source form, its possible print or online counterpart.

Vendor's Name: Sometimes the persons or groups responsible for supplying the information in publications on CD-ROM, diskette, and magnetic tape are also the publishers of the works. But many information providers choose instead to lease the data to vendors (e.g., Information Access, Silver Platter, UMI-ProA Quest) for distribution. It is important to state the vendor's name in the works-cited list, if it is given in the source, because the information provider may have leased electronic versions of the data to more than one vendor, and the versions may not be identical.

Publication Dates: Many databases published on CD-ROM, diskette, or magnetic tape are updated regularly (e.g., annually, quarterly). Updates add information and may also correct or otherwise alter information that previously appeared in the database. Therefore, a works-cited-list entry for material derived from such a database commonly contains the date of the document used, as indicated in the source, as well as the publication date (or date of the most recent updating) of the database.

A Non-periodical Publication on CD-ROM, Diskette, or Magnetic Tape

Many publications on CD-ROM, diskette, or magnetic tape are issued as books are – that is, without a plan to update or otherwise revise the work regularly. Cite a non-periodical publication on CD-ROM, diskette, or magnetic tape as a book, but add a description of the medium of publication. Since the information provider and the publisher are usually the same for such publications, no vendor's name appears, and only one publication date is given. The typical works-cited-list entry for the source consists of the following items:

1. Author's name (if given). If only an editor, a compiler, or a translator is identified, cite that person's name, followed by the appropriate abbreviation (ed., comp., trans)
2. Title of the Publication (highlighted)
3. Name of the editor, compiler, or translator (if relevant)
4. Publication medium (CD-ROM, Diskette, or Magnetic tape)
5. Edit, release, or version (if relevant)
6. Place of Publication
7. Name of the publisher
8. Date of Publication e.g., Braunmuller, A.R., ed., **Macbeth.** By William Shakespeare. CD-ROM. New York: Voyager, 1994, **English Poetry Full-Text Database.** Magnetic tape. Rel. 2. Cambridge. Eng.: Chadwyck-Healey, 1993

Material from a Periodically Published Database on CD-ROM

Many periodicals (journals, magazines, newspapers) and periodically published reference works, such as annual bibliographies and collections of abstracts, are published both in print and on CD-ROM as databases or as parts of databases. To cite such a work, begin with the publication data for the printed source or printed analogue, as identified in the CD-ROM publication.

1. Author's name (if given)
2. Publication information for the printed source or printed analogue (including title and date of print publication)
3. Title of the database (highlighted)
4. Publication medium (CD-ROM)
5. Name of the vendor (if relevant)
6. Electronic publication date e.g., Coates, Steve. "Et Tu, Cybernetica Machina User?" **New York Times** 28 Oct. 1996, late ed., D4. **New York Times Ondisc**. CD-ROM. UMI-Proquest. Dec. 1996. Danzey, Leigh Ann. "The Price of Success: An Analysis of Funding Top Ten men's and Women's Programs in Comparative Sports." DAI 5B (1997) : 795A. Florida. State U, 1997. **Dissertation Abstracts Ondisc**. CD-ROM. UMI-ProQuest. Mar. 1998.

   (Gibaldi 2000)

Foot notes, End notes, Text notes

Foot notes, end notes, Text notes and bibliographical entries are ways of documenting the sources investigated and acknowledging the help received from others. Failure to provide documentation can weaken one's argument. Failure to acknowledge the help received from others in the form of information, ideas and composed material incorporated into one's report can constitute plagiarism – copying material directly from any source, or simply paraphrasing such material and submitting it as one's own. This is also known as literary theft. Institutions promoting scholarly research and writing therefore treat plagiarism as a very serious matter. Depending upon the extent of plagiarizing, punishment can vary from a severe reprimand up to expulsion and disqualification. More broadly, persons who engage in plagiarism will undermine and ultimately destroy their reputation and professional potential. For such reasons, proper acknowledgement of sources is necessary as a matter of intellectual honesty and personal integrity. Material taken directly from another source should be acknowledged by the use of quotation marks and a footnote, end note or a text note. Material paraphrased from other sources should also be acknowledged in a similar fashion (Mabry, 1999).

The basic rule for preparing reference and bibliography entries is clarity and consistency. An entry should be clear so that a reader will know the exact source to which reference is made. Entries should be consistent to avoid confusion which might arise if entries are given in different formats. Foot notes are placed at the bottom of a page of text and separated from the text by a short line. End notes are placed at the end of a short research report and at the end of each chapter in a thesis or dissertation. Text notes and endnotes are associated primarily with the author-title system of giving references, although they are sometimes also used with the author-date system for other purposes. Text notes are associated with the author-date system of giving references.

Use of 'ibid' and "op.cit"

"*ibid.*" and "*op.cit.*" are two of the most commonly used abbreviations in foot notes and end notes. These abbreviations are not normally used in text notes and their usage in the author-date system of documentation normally occurs. Properly used, "ibid." and "*op.cit.*" are efficient ways of providing needed information in brief and simplified ways. 'ibid' refers to the reference just referred already or above so only the reference page to be noted along with "*ibid.*" In the case of "*op.cit*" the reference has already appeared elsewhere and hence along with "*op.cit*" the name of the author and the page should be given. The following eight sample footnotes / endnotes illustrate their primary usage:

1. Kurien, C.T., 1992, **The Economy: An Interpretive Introduction,** Sage Publications, New Delhi, 20.
2. *Ibid.,* 24.
3. *Ibid.*
4. Pramit Chaudhuri, 1978 **The Indian Economy: Poverty and Development** Vikas Publishing House, New Delhi, 233.
5. Kurien, *op. cit.,* 25.
6. Kurien, C.T., 1978, **Poverty, Planning and Social Transformation,** Allied Publishers, Bombay, 33.

7. Kurien, The Economy . . . , *op. cit.,* 221.
8. *Ibid.,* 350 – 351.

Common Abbreviations

As a general rule it is preferable to avoid the use of abbreviations in the text. However, abbreviations are useful in foot notes, end notes, text notes and bibliographies to provide information with economy in the use of space. Listed below are some of the commonly used abbreviations, shown in their standard form, along with their meaning. For those which are abbreviations of foreign words, their full form is given within parentheses. Note that those italicized should normally be italicized or underlined (following the practice that foreign words and their abbreviated forms are italicized or underlined – except when part of a quotation in that language, or when the word has become generally accepted in the English language). Also, those capitalized should always be capitalized, while those not capitalized here should be capitalized only when they are used to begin a sentence, foot note or endnote. The abbreviation "loc. Cit" (= loco citato, in the place cited) is not included in the list below because it is no longer recommended – it has often been incorrectly used and its purpose can normally be better served by other abbreviations such as "ibid." and "op. cit."

Since the following abbreviations are in standard use, it is not necessary to give their meaning when using them. Obviously, where standard abbreviations are available, these should be used. When none of the commonly accepted abbreviations will meet a writer's needs, the writer may develop his or her own abbreviations. As an aid to the reader, such abbreviations, along with their full meaning, should be shown in a "List of Abbreviations" in the preliminaries. As far as possible, the meaning of such abbreviations should be self-evident so as to minimize the need for the reader to refer to the List of Abbreviations.

anon.	= anonymous
art., arts.	= article, articles
ca. (circa)	= about (used to give an approximate date. e.g., "ca.1856")
cf. (confer)	= compare (one source with another; not to

	be used in place of "see" or "see also")
chap., chaps.	= chapter, chapters.
Col., cols.	= column, columns
Comp., comps.	= compiler, compilers
e.g., (exempli gratia)	= for example (one illustration from among several of the same class)
ed., eds.,	= editor, editors, edition, editions
2nd ed., 3rd ed.	= second edition, third edition
Et al. (et alit)	= and others (usually used to mean 'and other authors'. Note that a full stop is not placed after "et", as "et" is not an abbreviation.)
etc., (et cetera)	= and others of the same class, and so forth (but usage in scholarly writings is discouraged because of indefiniteness)
f., ff.	= and the following page(s) (but, mention of the exact pages is preferable – e.g., "pp. 42-49" rather than "pp. 42 ff.")
Fig., figs.,	= figure, figures
Ibid., (ibidem)	= same source / same work as cited in the immediately preceding foot note / end note.
i.e., (id est)	= that is to say (used to introduce a more complete, specific or alternative rendering of the immediately preceding point)
infra	= below (refers to a later part of the text; "see below" is generally preferable)
!, l!	= line, lines (but often best to spell out to avoid being mistakenly read as the numbers one and eleven)
lit.,	= literally
MS, MSS	= manuscript, manuscripts
N. B. (Nota bene)	= note carefully (give special attention to)

n., nn.,	= note, notes (referring to footnotes or endnotes)
n.d.,	= no date of publication given
n.p.,	= no place of publication given, no publisher given
no., nos.	= number, numbers
op. cit. (opera citato)	= in the work cited (a work previously cited in the same research report; may be used where full citation was given within previous 2-3 pages; otherwise, it is preferable to give author's name and a short form of the title)
p., pp.,	= page, pages
para., paras.	= paragraph, paragraphs
passim	= here and there (at various places in the same work– e.g., "pp. 82, 104, passim")
pt., pts.,	= part, and parts
rev.,	= revised, revised by, revision
sec., secs.	= section, sections
[sic]	= thus (used to indicate that an error in a quoted passages was in the original; placed immediately after the error; see example on p.71)
supra	= above (refers to a previous portion of the text; "see above" is generally preferable)
s.v. (sub verbo,	= under the word (or heading; used for making reference to listings in sub voce) encyclopedias and dictionaries; for an example, see page 164, number 24
trans.	= translator, translated by
v., vv.,	= verse. Verses
viz., (videlicet)	= namely (used to introduce an amplification or explanation of an immediately preceding point)

vs. (versus = against

vol., vols. = volume, volumes, as in vol.4, vols. 1-4

Compiling a Working Bibliography

A record of sources for research is called a Working Bibliography. The working bibliography will eventually evolve into the list of works cited that appears at the end of the research presentation. When the scholar adds sources to the working bibliography, let him be sure to enter all the publication particulars needed for the works-cited list.

The information to be recorded depends on the kind of sources used.

1. Book

1. Author's full name (last name first).
2. Year of Publication.
3. Full title (including any subtitle).
4. Edition (if the book is a second or later edition).
5. Number of volume and the total number of volumes (if the book is a multi volume work).
6. Place of publication.
7. Shortened form of the publishers name [e.g., Budden, Julian. 1992 The Operas of Verdi. rev. ed. 3 Vols. Clarendon, Oxford.

2. Article in a Scholarly Journal

1. Author's name.
2. Year of Publication.
3. Title of the article.
4. Title of the journal.
5. Volume number.
6. Inclusive page numbers of the article (i.e., the number of page on which the article begins, a hyphen and the number of the page on which the article ends.) e.g., Vartanev, Anri. 1991, "Television as Spectacle and Myth".

   Journal of communication 41: 162 – 71.

3. Newspaper or Magazine Article

1. Author's name.
2. Year of publication.
3. Title of the article.
4. Title of the periodical.
5. Inclusive page numbers of the article. e.g., Shea. Christopher. 1993, "The Limits of Free Speech". Chronicle of Higher Education 1 Dec.1993: A 37–38.

4. Internet Sources

1. Author's name.
2. Title of the document.
3. Title of the scholarly project, database, periodical or professional or personal site.
4. Number of the editor of the scholarly project or database.
5. Date of electronic publication or last update.
6. Name of the institution or organization sponsored or associated with site.
7. Date when one accessed the source.
8. Network address or URI. E.g., Oaklay. John H., March 1997, "The Achilles Printers". The Perseus Project. ed., Cregory Crane. Tufts. V. 14 May 1998.

   <http:/www.pwerseu.stuftsed/secondary/printeressays/Achillestoc.html>

APPENDIX

A BASIC GLOSSARY OF TERMS USED IN RESEARCH

Bias: The conscious or sub-conscious influence of a researcher on what and how research is carried out. Bias can/will affect: the choice of topics/problems/questions to research; research planning and design; methods of data collection, e.g., interviewing, data analysis, interpretation of results, discussion and conclusion.

Biased sample: The result of a sampling strategy which deliberately includes or excludes certain individual or groups. A sample may be biased for good reasons.

Case study: The study of single 'cases' or 'units of analysis', e.g., a person, an event, a group, an organization, a classroom, a town, a family ... Commonly used in law, medicine and education. Howard Becker, the American sociologist, urges that case-study researchers should continually ask: 'What is this a case of?' Case study is often chosen to explore how or why questions and situations are in their natural setting when the researcher is not attempting to control or intervene in them. Cases are often chosen to deepen understanding of an event, a problem, an issue, a theory or a model.

Cognition: The act of knowing or understanding; knowledge can be understanding that or knowledge how and in some cases knowledge why. Thus the process of cognition can involve skill, knowledge or understanding.

Control group: The group of people (or plants or animals) in an experiment who do not experience that treatment given to an experimental group –allegedly as identical as possible to the experimental group. In theory, the purpose of a control group is to show what would have happened to the experimental group if it had not been exposed to the experimental treatment.

Deconstruction: A way of examining texts (i.e., 'taking apart'). By searching for the unspoken or unformulated messages of a text, it can be shown to be saying something more than or different to what it appears or purports to say. Texts say many different things, i.e., there is not one essential meaning.

Dependent variable: The thing/phenomenon which one studies or measures in a controlled experiment; the variable changed or influenced by an experimental treatment.

Discourse analysis: A general term used to encompass a range of approaches to analyzing talk, text, writing etc. mainly concerned with analyzing what is being communicated and how, looking for codes, rules and signs in speech or text.

Document analysis: The strategies and procedures for analyzing and interpreting the documents of any kind important for the study of a particular area. Documents might be public, e.g., government documents, media cutting, television scripts, minutes of meetings; or private, e.g., letters, diaries, school records, memoirs, interview transcripts, transcripts prepared from vide records or photographs.

Empirical research: (As opposed to deskwork or 'armchair' research) inquiry involving first-hand data collection, e.g., by interviewing, observation, questionnaire. One can do empirical research without being an 'empiricist' (like 'positivist', a term of abuse).

Epistemology: The study of the nature and validity of human knowledge, e.g. the difference between knowledge and belief. The two traditional camps have been: rationalism, which stresses the role of human reason in knowing; and empiricism which stresses the importance of sensory perception. Immanuel Kant argued that most knowledge is a synthesis or combination of the two approaches.

Ethnography: A methodology with its roots in anthropology (literally, the study of people); aims to describe and interpret human behaviour within a certain culture; uses extensive field work and participant observation, aiming to develop rapport and empathy with people studied.

Experimental group: The group of people in a controlled experiment who experience the experimental treatment or intervention.

Formative evaluation: Evaluation carried out in the early or intermediate stages of a programme, a course or an intervention while changes can still be made; the formative evaluation shapes and informs those changes. Summative evaluation is carried out at the end of a program or intervention to assess its impact.

Generalisability: The extent to which research findings in one context can be transferred or applied to other contexts or settings. No findings, even those based on a statistical sample, can be generalized with complete certainty.

Grounded theory: Theory emerging from the data collected in a research study by the process of induction.

Hawthorne effect: Initial improvement in performance following any newly introduced change – an effect or problem which the researcher needs to be wary of if making an intervention into a natural setting, e.g., introducing new teaching methods to assess their impact.

Hermeneutics: The art or science of interpretation, a term first coined by William Dilthey. The term may now apply to the interpretation of a text, a work of art, human behaviour, discourse, documents and so on. Hans-Georg Gadamer proposed hermeneutics as a form of practical philosophy or methodology; the aim is to interpret and understand the meaning of social actions and social settings.

Hypothesis: A tentative proposal or unproved theory, put forward for examination and testing; it can be used to guide and direct research along certain lines with certain procedures to 'put the hypothesis to the test'.

Induction: The process of inferring a general law from the observation of particular instances. David Hume (1711-76) talked of the 'fallacy of induction': One can never be certain of a general law, e.g., 'All swans are white', based on particular observation, e.g. seeing numerous white swans.

Instrument: Any technique or tool that a researcher uses, e.g., a questionnaire, an interview schedule, observation framework etc.

Interview schedule: A set of questions used in interviewing; questions may range from closed to open, in which respondents express their views and experiences openly and freely. Interviews may range from unstructured to semi-structured to completely structured (a face-to-face questionnaire), i.e., from totally open to completely predetermined.

Interpretative approach: Argues that human behaviour can only be explained by referring to the subjective states of the people acting in it; this approach can be applied to the study of social actions/ activity social life can only be explained by the examination of observable entities.

Logical positivism: A philosophy developed between 1922 and 1940 by the 'Vienna Circle' based on the earlier philosophies of Augusta Comte and the empiricist David Hume; argues that the only meaningful knowledge is that based on and verifiable by, direct sense experience. Hence, any descriptive statement that cannot be empirically verified by sense observation is meaningless. This doctrine would rule out theology, metaphysics and hermeneutics.

Logical positivism is now largely discredited but is often (wrongly) confused with positivism and with 'being scientific'; all three are based on different ideas.

Longitudinal research: Research in which data are collected and analyzed on the same individuals or the same organizations, e.g., schools, colleges or the same groups, e.g., families, at different points over an extended period of time; for example, on a carefully chosen sample of children/youth/adults at the ages of 7, 14, 21, 28, 35,42.

Methodology: The study of the methods, design and procedures used in research.

N: the number of people or subjects, studies or samples in a research project; e.g., N = 1, signifies a single case study.

Ockham's razor: After William of Ockham's law of economy: entities are not to be multiplied beyond necessity. A law originally applied to ontology but can be usefully stretched further, e.g. chopping excessive words from a paper or thesis.

Ontology: The study or theory of 'what is', i.e., the characteristics of reality.

Paradigm: A term which became fashionable following Thomas Kuhn's book The Structure of Scientific Revolutions; now commonly over-used to mean perspective/ view of the world, methodological position, viewpoint, community of researchers, cognitive framework and so on. Researchers often speak of 'the qualitative and quantitative paradigms', as if they were separate and mutually exclusive; or the 'positive paradigm' as a widely held and dangerous tendency.

Participant observation: A methodology or practice with its roots in early twentieth-century anthropology; it entails a researcher spending a prolonged period of time participating in the daily activities of a community or a group, e.g., a tribe, a gang, a school, the armed forces; and observing their practices, norms , customs and behavior (either overtly or covertly). The researcher becomes socialized into the group being studied. The method therefore demands that a fine line be drawn between empathy/ rapport with the group and over-familiarity/total involvement. As a method it may lead to both practical concerns, e.g., safety and ethical concerns, e.g., pretending to be something we are not, in some situations.

Positivism: The belief that all true knowledge is based on observable phenomena; NOT the same as 'scientific' which does deal in unobservable, theoretical entities. 'You positivist!' is often used for verbal abuse.

Postmodernism: A widely used term, impossible to define, encompassing a broad range of amorphous ideas, e.g., it signals the end of universal truths, totalistic explanations and 'grand narratives', giving way to little narratives (petits recits) and local knowledge, adequate for particular communities. Key words are: difference, heterogeneity, fragmentation and indeterminacy.

Purposive/purposeful sampling: Sampling done with deliberate aims in mind as opposed to a random sample or one chosen purely for its convenience and accessibility. Cases or sites may be chosen purposefully for a variety of reasons, e.g., for being typical or extreme or deviant or unique or exemplary or revelatory. Hence the cases or sites are selected with certain criteria in mind.

Qualitative: Of or relating to quality or kind ('qualis'[Greek]); adjective describing methods or approaches which deal with non numeric data, i.e., words rather than numbers.

Quantitative: Of quantity or number; methods or approaches which deal with numeric data, amounts or measurable quantities, i.e., numbers. A false dichotomy is often drawn between a qualitative and a quantitative 'paradigm', as if the two approaches could not be used to complement and enrich each other. Also, use of quantitative data is often (wrongly) labeled 'positivism'.

Random sample: Sample of the members of a given population drawn in such a way that every member of that population has an equal chance of being selected, e.g., every tenth name in a long list. Random sampling should eliminate the operation of bias in selecting a sample. The term 'population' means the entire group from which the sample is selected, e.g., every student in a particular school/college. The population itself depends on the focus and scope of the research.

Reflexivity: Commonly used to describe a test or examination. The term is also used in connection with research methods in order to estimate the degree of confidence in the data. Reliability refers to the extent to which a test or technique functions consistently and accurately by yielding the same results at different times or when used by different researchers.

Research is said to be reliable if it can be repeated or replicated by another researcher and/or at a different time.

Sample: The smaller number of cases, units or sites selected from a much larger population. (universe). Some samples are assumed to be representative of the entire population, i.e., generalisable from, but this can never be done with certainty.

Theory: An idea, model or principle used to explain why observed phenomena happen as they do; theory seeks patterns, relationships, correlations, associations or connections, e.g., between aspects of behavior and factors which might affect it or explain it.

Some theories may be predictive, i.e. capable of predicting certain outcomes given certain factors or circumstances, as well as explanatory. For example, poverty might be a good 'predictor' of low educational achievement. The search for a belief in direct causality, i.e., X causes Y, is now highly debatable in modern science and in research.

Triangulation: The business of giving strength or support to findings/conclusions by drawing on evidence from other sources: (i) other methods (methodological triangulation), e.g., interviews, observations, questionnaires; (ii) other researchers; (iii) other times, e.g., later in a project; (iv) other places, e.g., different regions. Thus the same area of study is examined from more than one vantage point, cf. surveying a site.

Trustworthiness: A criterion offered by Lincoln and Guba (1985) as an alternative to the traditional 'reliability' and 'validity' in judging research. Trustworthiness has four parts: (i) credibility; (ii) transferability (cf. external validity); (iii) dependability; (iv) conformability (the later two being parallel to reliability).

Validity: The extent or degree to which an inquiry, a method, test, technique or instrument measures what it sets out or purports to measure, e.g., an intelligence test, an interview, a questionnaire. No instrument could ever be said to be valid with total certainty.

External validity is the extent to which the findings or conclusions of a piece of research could be generalized to apply to contexts/situations other than those in which the data have been collected. Validity can be seen as a measure of the confidence in, credibility of or plausibility of a piece of research.

Variable: A measurable or non-measurable characteristic which varies from one individual or organization to another. Some may be qualitative, others quantitative, i.e., expressible as numbers. Age, gender, ability, personality characteristics, 'intelligence' are a few examples of human variables. In some approaches, the researcher attempts to control or manipulate variables; in other approaches the researcher studies or observes them in their natural setting without deliberately intervening.

BIBLIOGRAPHY

Abrams, M.A.., *Social Surveys and Social Action,* London: Heinemann, 1951.

Abreo, Desmond, *Ideology and Process of Participatory Evaluation,* New Delhi, Indian Social Institute. 2000.

American Psychological Association, *Ethical principles in the Conduct of*

Research with Human Participants, Washington, D.C.: A PA, 1973.

Ann. Pickett, Ann A. Laster and Katherine E. Staples. *Teaching English: Writing, Reading and Speaking,* 8th ed. New York, Addison Wesley Longman. 2001

Anderson, Jonathan, Berry H. Durston and Millicent Poole, *Thesis and Assignment*

Writing, Sydney: John Wiley and Sons, Australia, 1970; New Delhi: Wiley Eastern, 1970 (Indian reprint).

Arthur, Maurice, *Philosophy of Scientific Investigation,* Baltimore: John Hopkins University press, 1943.

Aruna Goel, S.L. Goes, *Encyclopedia of Higher Education in the 21st Century,* New Delhi, Deep & Deep publication Pvt. Ltd., 2005.

Atkinson, J., *A Handbook for Interviewers,* (Govt. Social Survey No. M 136), London: H.M.S.O., 1967.

Aydelotte, W.O., Bouge, A.G., and Fogel R.W, eds. *The Dimensions of Quantitative Research in History,* Princeton, N.J. Princeton N.J., Princeton University Press, 1972.

Babbie, Earl R, *The Basics of Social Research,* 8th ed., Belmont, California, Wordsworth Publishing Company, 1998.

————, *The Practice of Social Research*, 8th ed, Belmont, California, Wordsworth Publishing Company, 1998.

Ballou, Stephen, V., *A Model for Theses and Research Papers,* Boston: Houghton Mifflin, 1970.

Barzun, Jacques and Henry F. Graff, *The Modern Researcher*, 2nd ed. New York,

Harcourt, Brace & World, 1970.

Berelson, Bernard, *Content Analysis in communication Research,* Glencoe, III: Free Press, 1942.

Bereson, Conrad and Raymond Colton, *Research and Report Writing for Business and Economics*, New York: Random House, 1971 Chapters 8 to 17.

Berkhofer, Robert F, *A Behavioral Approach to Historical Analysis*, New York, Free Press, 1969.

Bernstein, Jeremy, *The Analytical Engine: Computers, Past, Present and Future,* New York, Random House, 1964.

Berry, Ralph, *How to write a Research Paper*: Oxford: Pergamon Press, 1966.

Best, John W, Research in Education, New Delhi,.Prentice Hall of India Pvt. Ltd. 1982,

Beteille, Andre and T.N. Madan, eds. *Encounter and Experience, Personal Account of Field Work,* Delhi Vikas, 1975.

Bindrawan Lal, Research Methodology, Jaipur, ABT Publishers. 2002.

Blalock, Hubert M., *Casuals Inference in nonexperimental Research*, Chapel Hill, University of North Carolina Press, 1964.

Booth, Wayne C, Gregory G, Colomb and Joseph M. Williams, *The Craft of Research*, University of Chicago, 1995.

Bowles, Edmond A., *Computers n Humanistic Research: Readings and Perspectives,* Englewood Cliffs, N.J., Prentice Hall, 1967.

Brog, Walter. R. *Educational Research: An Introduction*, New York, David Mckay Company, Inc. 1963.

Bulmer, Martin, "Interviewing and Fields Organization", in Martin

Bulmer and Donald P. Warwick, *Social Research in Developing Countries,* New York; Wiley & Sons Ltd., 1983.

Campbell D.T. and Stanley, J.C., *Experimental and Quasi-Experimental Design for Research,* Chicago, Rand McNally. 1966.

Campbell, William Giles, and Ballou, Stephen Vaghan, *Form and style. Theses, Reports, Term Papers,* Boston: Houghton Mifflin Company, 1974.

Campbell, William G, *Form and Style in Thesis Writing*, Cambridge, Massachusetts: Houghton Mifflin Co., 1975.

Carmines, Edward G., and Richard A. Zeller, *Reliability and Validity Assessment,* Beverly Hills, Calif., Sage University Papers, 1979.

Chandra, Arvinda and T.P.Saxena, *Style Manuel for Writing Thesis, Dissertations and Papers in Social Sciences,* New Delhi: Metropolitan Book Co., 1979.

Childe, V.Gordon, *Piecing Together the Past: methods and Theories of Archeology,* New York, Praeger, 1969.

Claire Seltiz, Lawerence S. Wrightsman, Stuart W. Cook, *Research Methods in Social Relations,* New York, Holt, Rinchart and Winston.. 2007.

Claus A. Moser and G. Kalton, *Survey Methods in Social Investigation*, London, Heinemann Educational Books Ltd. 1976.

Cochran, William G., *Sampling Techniques* New York: John Wiley & Sons, 1963.

Cohen, Morris R., and Ernest Nagel, *An Introduction to Logic and Scientific Method,* New York: Harcourt, Brace, 1934.

Conway, Freda, *Sampling: An Introduction for Social Scientists,* London: George Allen and Unwin, 1967.

Cook, Stuart, "Ethical Implications", in Kidder, Louise H., AND Judd, Charles, M, *Research Methods in Social Relations,* New York: CBS Publishing Japan Ltd., 1986.

Deming, W.E., *Sample Design in Business Research,* New York: John Wiley & Sons, 1960.

Denzin, Norman K and Yvonna S. Lincoln, eds. *Handbook of*

Qualitative Research, Thousand oaks/ London/ New Delhi: Sage, 1994. (hardback); 1998 (3 vol. paperback ed.).

Doby, John T., (ed) *An Introduction to Social Research.* Harrisburg, Pa.: Stackpole C., 1954.

Dollar, C.M. and Jensen, R.J., *Historical Guide to Statistics: Quantitative Analysis and Historical Research,* New York, Holt, Reiehart and Winston, 1971.

Dunaway, David K. and Willa K Baum. Eds. *Oral History, An Interdisciplinary Approach,* Nashville; American Association for State and Local History in cooperation with the Oral History Association, 1984; 2nd ed. Walnut Greek, California; AltaMira Press, 1996.

Edros, Paul L., *Professional Mail Surveys,* New York: Mc Graw-Hill Book Co., 1970.

Edwards, Allen L., *Experimental Design in Psychological Research,* New York: Holt Rinehart and Winston, 1972.

Emerson, Robert M., Rachel I, Fretz and Linda I. Shaw, *Writing Ethnographic Fieldnotes*, Chicago, 1995.

Fernandas Walter and Philip Vegas, *Participatory and Conventional Research Methodologies,* New Delhi; Indian Social Institute, 1985.

Festinger, Leon and Katz, Daniel, *Research Methods in the Behavioral Science,* New York: Holt, Rinehart and Winston, 1953.

Fox, David J., *The Research Process in Education,* New York: Holt, Rinehart and Winston, 1969 (Chapter1&2).

Gibaldi, Joseph, *MLA Handbook for Writers of Research Papers,* 4th ed., New York: The Modern Language Association of America, 1995.

——————, MLA *Handbook for Writer of Research Papers*, Fifth edition, New Delhi, Affiliated East-West Press Pvt. Ltd. 2000.

Ghosh B.N, *Scientific Method & Social Research*, 4th ed., New Delhi, Sterling Publishers Pvt. Ltd. 1994.

Giles, G.B., *Marketing, 2nd ed.,* New York, Macdonald & Evans Ltd., 1974.

Goode, W. J. and Hatt, P. K. *Methods in Social Research*, New York, Mc Graw – Hill Book Company. 1952.

Greenwood, D. and M. Levin, *Introduction to Action Research*, London, SCM Press. 1998.

Green, Paul, and Tull, Donald, *Research for marketing Decisions*, Englewood Cliffs, N.J., Prentice-Hall, 1970 (Chapter1&2).

Guilford, J.P. *Fundamental Statistics in Psychology and Education,* 4th ed., New York, McGraw – Hill Book Company, 1965.

Guilford, J.P., Fundamental Statistics in Psychology and Education, 4th Hagedorn, Robert and Sanford Labovitz, Introduction to Social Research, New York: McGraw –Hill, 1971.

Hatch, Elvin, *Theories of Man and Culture,* New York, Columbia University Press, 1973.

Heller, Louis G, *Communicational Analysis and Methodology for Historians,* New York, University Press, 1971.

Helmstader, G.C., *Research concepts in Human Behaviour,* New York: Appleton-Century-Crofts, 1970 (Chapter2-4)

House, E. R, *Educational Researcher*, London, Widenfield and Nicholson. 1978.

Hornby, A.S., *Oxford Advanced Learner's Dictionary of current English, Sally Wehmeier Michael Ashby, ed., 6th ed., New Delhi, Indira Printers, 2000.*

http://en.wikipedia.org/wiki/chi-square-test

http://www.etsu.edu/haleyd/engl15939/ejournal/lewis.htm (Retrieved on 12.09.2006).

http://en.wikipedia.org/wiki/Evaluation

http://www.gslis.utexaa.edu/~wyllys/IRLISMaterial/evaluatngres.html

http://www.qse.harvard.edu/hfrp/eval/issue2/eval.html

http://en.wikipedia.org/wiki/evaluation (Retrieved on 12. 09. 2006).

http://www.gslis.utexas.edu/~wyllys/IRLISMaterial/evaluatingres.html (Retrieved on 12. 09. 2006).

Helmstadter, G.C., *Research Concepts in Human Behaviour,* New York: Appleton-Century-Crofts, 1970.

Hirchi, T., and Selvin, H.C., *Delinquency Research:* An Appraisal of Analytic Methods, New York: Free Press, 1967.

Huck, Suchyler W., Cormier, William H., and Bounds, William G., *Reading Statistics and Research,* New York: Harper Row, 1974.

Hyman, H.H., Cobb, W.I. and others, *Interviewing in Social Research,* Chicago, The University of Chicago Press, 1954.

Jackson, E.T. knowledge shared, Philadelphia, Fortress Press, 1998.

Jagdish N.Sheth, *The Multivariate Revolution in Marketing Research*, Journal of Marketing, Vol. 35, No.1, 1971.

Jane E.Schukoske, *University News,* 45(48) November – December 2002.

Johnson, Janet Buttolph and Joslyn, Richard A., *Political Science Research Methods,* New Delhi: Prentice-Hall of India, 1989, Chapter 6.

John W.Best, *Research in Education,* New Delhi, Prentice Hall in India Pvt. Ltd., 1982.

Jonis, J. Harold, *The Business Research Paper,* New York: Hobbis, Dorman & Co., 1967.

Joseph, A. Antony, *Methodology for Research. Guide for Writing Dissertations, Theses and Scientific Papers,* Bangalore: Theological Publications of India, 1986.

Joseph Gibalidi, *MLA Handbook for writers of Research Papers*, 5th ed., New Delhi, Affiliated East – West Press Pvt. Ltd., 2000.

Jurabian, Kate L., *A Manual for Writers of Term Papers, Theses and Dissertations,* Chicago: University of Chicago Press, 1971

Kah, R.L., and Cannel, C.F., *The Dynamics of Interviewing: Theory, Technique and Cases,* New York: John Wiley & Sons, 1957.

Kahn, Robert I., and Cannel Charles F., *The Dynamic of Interviewing,* New York: John Wiley and Sons, 1957.

Kalyani T. S. *Tools of data Collection*: *The Schedule and*

Questionnaire, UGC Refresher course for University Teachers and Teachers, Thanjavur, Tamil University. 2004.

Kerliner Fred., N. *Foundations of Behavioral Research*: New York, Holt, Rinehart and Winston. 1973.

Kerlinger, F.N. and E. Pedhazer, *Multiple Regression in Behavioral Research,* New York: Holt, Rinehart and Winston, 1973.

Kerlinger, Fred N., *Foundations of Behavioural Research,* Delhi: Surjeet Publications, 1983 (Part 6&7).

Komidar, Joseph S., "Use of the Library", in Goode, William J., and Hatt, Paul K., *Methods in Social* Research, New York: Mc-Graw-Hill Book company, 1952,

Kothari, C.R, *Research Methodology, Methods and Techniques*, 2nd ed. New Delhi, Wiley Eastern, 1990.

Kothari C. R, *Research Methodology*, New Delhi, Wisha Prakashan. 2009.

Lal Bindrawan, *Research Methodology*, Jaipur, ABT Publishers, 2002.

Langer, William L, *"The Next Assignment*", American Historical Review, LXIII (January 1958), 283-304.

Lincoln Y.S, and Denzin K (eds,) *Handbook of Qualitative Research*, London, Thousand Oaks, Sage. 2000.

Marby, Hunter P, *A Manual for Researchers and Writers*, Bangalore, The Board of Theological Education of the Senate of Serampore College. 2004.

Mathur, Kuldeep and Harsh Sethi, eds., *Action Research for Development*, New Delhi: Indian Institute of Public Administration, 1983.

McCall, George J., and J.L. Simons, *Issues in Participant Observation,* Reading, M.A.: Addison- Wesley, 1969.

Merton, R.K., Fiske, M., and Kendall, P.L., *The Focused Interview: A Manual of Problems and Procedures,* Glencoe, III: Press, 1956.

Michael V.P., *Research Methodology in Management*, Bombay, Himalaya Publishing House. 1985.

Mies, Marie, "*Towards a methodology of feminist research*" In

Theories of Women's Studies, Edited by Gloria Bowles and Renate Duelli Klein. London: Routledge, 1983.

Miller, Delbert C., *Hand book of Research Design and Social Measurement,* New York: Longman, 1983.

Moser, Claus A., *Survey Methods in social Investigation*, London, Heinmann Educational Books Ltd. 1999.

Monash University, Ph.D. Hand book, Australia, Victoria, 2009.

Mudrick, Robert G., *Business Research Concept and Practice,* Scranton, Pa.: International Textbook.1969.

Murthy, M.N. *Sampling Theory and Methods,* Calcutta: Stastical Publishing Society, 1967.

Nielsen, Joyce McCarl, ed. *Feminist Research Methods*, Exemplary Readings in the Parsons C, J., *Theses and Project Work,* London: George Allen and Unwin, 1973.

Oppenheim, A.N., *Questionnaire Design and Attitude Measurement,* London: Heinemann Educational Books, 1973.

Parten, B. Mildred, Surveys, Polls and Samples, New York: Harper & Brothers. 1959.

Parten, .S, *Surveys, Polls and Samples: Practical Procedures*, New York: Harper & Brothers, Publishers, 1950.

Patton, M, *Qualitative Evaluation Methods*, Oxford, Clarendon Press. 1990.

Paul V. Anderson, *Ethical Issues in the Conduct of Person-Based Composition Research*, New York, John Wiley & Sons. 1998.

Pitt, David, C, *Historical Sources in Anthropology and Sociology*, New York, Holt, Rinehart, and Winston, 1971.

Phillips, Bernard S., *Social Research,* New York: Macmillan Co.: 1971, Chapters 13-16.

Raj, Des, *The Design of Sample Surveys,* New York: McGraw-Hill, 1972.

Raj, Hans. *Theory and Practice in Social Research*, Third ed., Delhi, Surjeet publications. 2005.

Ram Ahuja, *Research Methodology*, New Delhi, Rawart Publications. 2003.

Richardson, S.A.,Dohrewend, B.S., and Klien, D., *Interviewing: Its forms and Functions,* New York: Basic Books, 1965.

Rubin, Herbert J., *Applied Social Research,* Columbus: Northern Illinois University, 1983.

Sadhu, A. N. & Singh Amarjit, *Research Methodology in Social Sciences*, Bombay, Himalaya Publishing Houses. 1980.

Saravanavel P, *Research Methodology*, 6th ed. Allahabad, Kitab Mahal, 2005.

Selltiz, Claire et al., *Research Methods in Social Relations,* New York: Holt, Rinehart and Winston, 1959 (Chapter 1&4).

Seltiz, Claire. *Research Methods in Social Relations*, New York, Holt, Rinehart and Winston. 1976.

Shah, Vimal P. *Reporting Research*, Ahmedabad: Rachava Prakasan, 1977.

Sinha, Raghuvir, *Content Analysis, A New Method in Social Research*, New Delhi; Ambica Publications; 1980.

Simon, Julian L., and Paul Burstein, *Basic Research Methods in Social Science,* New York Random House, 1985.

Sjoberg, Gideon (ed.), *Ethics, Politics and Social Research,* Cambridge, Mass.: Schaenkman publishing, 1967.

Sjoberg, Gideon and Roger Nett, *A Methodology for Social Research*, New York: Harper & Row, 1968, Jaipur: Rawat Publications, 1977.

Som, R.K., *A Manual of Sampling Techniques*, London: Heinemann Educational Books, 1973.

Srinivas, M.N., A.M. Shah and E.A.Ramaswamy, eds. *The Fieldworker and the Field*, Delhi, Oxford University Press, 1979.

Stephen, F.F., and McCarthy, P.J., *Sampling Opinions*: *An Analysis of Survey Procedure*, New York: John Wiley & Sons, 1958.

Stephen, Isaac and William B Michael, *Handbook in Research and Evaluation*, San Diego, California, Edits Publishers. 1982.

Stufflebeam, D. L., & Webster, W.J. *Educational Evaluation and Policy Analysis.*

London, Allen and Unwin. 1980. Sukhatme, P.V., and Sukhatme, B.V., *Sampling Theory of Surveys with applications,* London: Asia Publishing House, 1970.

Survey Research Center, *Field Methods in Sample Interviewers".,* Ann Arbor, Michigan: University of Michigan, 1951.

Survey Research Center, *Interviewer's Manual,* An Arbor: Institute of Social Research, University of Michigan, 1969.

Tashakkori A and Teddlie C; Eds., *Hand Book of Mixed Research in Social and Behavioral Sciences,* California, Thousand Oaks. 2003.

Thorndike R.M., *Correlational Procedures for Research,* New York: Gardener Pres, 1978.

Turabian, Kate L, *A Manuel for Writers of Term Papers, Theses and Dissertations*, 6th ed., Chicago: University of Chicago Press, 1996.

Van Dalen, D.B., *Understanding Educational Research* 4th ed., New York,. McGraw Hill. 1979.

Warwick, D., and Lininger C., *The Sample Survey: Theory and Practice,* New York; McGraw-Hill, 1975.

Warwick, Donald P., *"The Politics and Ethics of Field Research"*, in Bulmer, Martin and Warwick, Donald p., (Eds.) *Social Research in Developing Countries*, New York: John wiley & Sons, 1983.

William Emory C, *Business Research Methods*, Illinois, Richard D. Irwin, Inc. 1976.

Wilkinson, T. S. and Bhandarkar, P. L., *Methodology and Techniques of Social Research,* 11th ed., Mumbai, Himalaya Publishing House, 1994.

www.weizmann, ac.il / conferences, seegs

Yin, Robert K, *Case Study Research, Design and Methods*, 2nd ed., New delhi, Sage, 1989.

Young, Pauline V, *Scientific Social Survey and Research,* 4th ed., 1966. Reprint: New Delhi; Prentice Hall of India, 1975.